T0334701

Contents

ANTI-RACISM IN HIGHER EDUCATION

An Action Guide for Change

Edited by
Arun Verma

First published in Great Britain in 2022 by

Policy Press, an imprint of
Bristol University Press
University of Bristol
1–9 Old Park Hill
Bristol
BS2 8BB
UK
t: +44 (0)117 374 6645
e: bup-info@bristol.ac.uk

Details of international sales and distribution partners are available at
policy.bristoluniversitypress.co.uk

© Bristol University Press 2022

British Library Cataloguing in Publication Data
A catalogue record for this book is available from the British Library

ISBN 978-1-4473-6472-6 paperback
ISBN 978-1-4473-6473-3 ePub
ISBN 978-1-4473-6474-0 ePdf

The right of Arun Verma to be identified as editor of this work has been asserted by
him in accordance with the Copyright, Designs and Patents Act 1988.

Cover design: Robin Hawes
Front cover image: iStock/Andrey Danilovich
University Press and Policy Press use environmentally
responsible print partners.
Printed and bound in Great Britain by CMP, Poole

For my niece, nephew and all young people – this book serves to help ensure you don't experience the racial injustices we did in pursuit of a higher education.

Contents

List of abbreviations

ASC	Athena Swan Charter
BAME	Black, Asian and minority ethnic
BLM	Black Lives Matter
BoG	Board of Governors
ECU	Equality Challenge Unit
EDI	equality, diversity and inclusion
EEDI	equality/equity, diversity and inclusion
HE	higher education
HEIs	higher education institutions
HEPI	Higher Education Policy Institute
HR	Human Resources
NSS	National Student Survey
REC	Race Equality Charter
REF	research excellence framework
TEF	teaching excellence framework

Notes on contributors

Musharrat J. Ahmed-Landeryou has been Senior Lecturer at London South Bank University (LSBU) since 2002. She is a part-time PhD student on the topic of people-designed service improvement. She is Co-founder of BAMEOTUK, a network of occupational therapy students, practitioners and educators interested in changing the status quo of institutional racism in the profession and professional body, established June 2020. She is current rotating Co-chair of the BAME Strategic Advisory Group at the Institute of Health and Social Care at LSBU.

Anonymous One of the authors has asked to remain anonymous for their contribution.

Rashid Aziz is Senior Lecturer in Criminology at London South Bank University. His teaching focus is on hate crime and the media representation of crime. His research focuses on British Muslims and marriage as well as martial arts.

Parise Carmichael-Murphy is a PhD Education Student and Research Assistant at the Manchester Institute of Education, University of Manchester. She is concerned with understanding the social determinants of mental health and wellbeing, particularly within the context of education. She is interested in intersectional approaches to unpick social inequities, particularly concerning gender, race and age.

Briana Coles is educated in Molecular Biology, Pathology, Epidemiology and Biostatistics, and her research uses population-based audit data to advance understanding of the interactions between cancer and cardiovascular disease. She sits on a number of committees and boards pushing for equitable representation of Black women across all STEM fields.

Min Duchenski is Subject Leader for the Psychology PGCE at the Institute of Education, UCL. Prior to working in HE, she was a teacher of Psychology for 14 years in two large west London schools. In her second appointment she became Head of Psychology and was Subject Lead for the borough's school alliance (of all Heads of Psychology in local schools). She completed the National Professional Qualification for Senior Leadership but moved into HE before progressing into senior leadership. She has completed a Masters in Educational Neuroscience and is currently completing a PhD exploring the effects of trauma on mental health and wellbeing. She is also a member of the British Psychological Society.

Josephine Gabi is Senior Lecturer at Manchester Metropolitan University. Her research interests are in postcolonial critique, decoloniality, Black feminism and network theory, with particular focus on the restorative potential of hospitable and decolonial pedagogy as a critical orientation towards developing a sense of belonging in higher education.

Jitesh S. B. Gajjar is Professor of Applied Mathematics at the University of Manchester. He obtained his undergraduate and PhD degrees from Imperial College, then worked as a research scientist before taking up a lecturing post at the University of Exeter. He moved to Manchester in 1991. His research expertise is in fluid mechanics and he has published extensively, including co-authoring *Fluid Dynamics Volume 1* (2014).

Eileen Ggbagbo is an International Relations graduate from the London School of Economics.

Sonia Gomes is Librarian at the London School of Economics. She has a BSc in Environmental Science, an MA in Information Management Services and an AFHEA for teaching and supporting learning in HE. Her interests are information literacy and inclusive pedagogy. She is a member of the Staff BAME network and founder member of Library EDI Champions at the London School of Economics.

Manvir Kaur Grewal is Lecturer at the University of Westminster. Her research focuses on socio-legal theory, particularly in relation to inequalities in the legal profession and higher education. She is a part-time PhD student examining the lived experiences of female barristers in the context of sexual offences.

Claire Lee is from Boston in the United States. Upon graduating from her BA degree she spent some time working in Korea and travelling around Asia. She came to Nottingham for an MA degree and has stayed since. During her time in the UK, she has worked in the start-up sector, student recruitment at all levels, WP outreach and EDI. She is now based at the University of Sheffield, where she works in marketing and recruitment.

Manish Maisuria is Chair of the Staff BAME Forum, Co-chair of the Staff LGBT+ Forum, Co-lead for the Athena Swan SAT department and a Union Equalities Officer at the University of Leicester. He also acts as Action Group Lead for the University's LGBT+ Equality Action Group and is a member of the University's Race Equality Action Group.

Tamjid Mujtaba is Senior Research Fellow for the UCL Institute of Education. She is Principal Investigator for the Focus4Taps Evaluation, Module Leader for Advanced Research Theory and Practice, Co-investigator for Chemistry for All and Co-director for Broadening Secondary School Science.

Deya Mukherjee is EDI Advisor on race (staff side) at the University of Bristol, with a particular interest in moving away from models of envisioning oppression as 'unconscious' and arising from 'innate human tendencies', and instead finding ways to have uncomfortable conversations about historical and contemporary power dynamics, as a way of getting to the root of what it means to practise anti-oppression.

Zoe Nutakor is Charities and Outreach Officer for Durham's South College. She arrived at Durham after a long road and has since thrown herself into university life. As Senior Welfare Officer, she is taking the lead in embedding anti-racism into the college from the outset.

Jalpa Ruparelia is Research Fellow at the University of Nottingham working on International Development projects and her own research. Following a teaching career in schools, colleges and HE, she led initial teacher education programmes and embarked on her doctoral journey as a part-time student.

Shaminder Takhar is Associate Professor in Sociology at London South Bank University. She leads the Race, Gender and Sexualities Research Group and is Chair of the School Ethics Panel and the staff network, EquiNet. Her research and publications are centred around race, gender, sexuality and social justice. She is an Editorial Board Member of the journals *Sociology* and *Sociological Research Online*, and has recently edited a special issue on nationalism's futures.

Pamela Thomas is on a six-month secondment as the Interim EDI Manager at London South Bank University. In her previous role she was the Senior Learning Developer in the Skills for Learning Centre at the Centre for Research Informed Teaching.

Arun Verma is a leading Impact Specialist in developing and implementing intersectionality approaches to anti-racism, equality and diversity practice, policy and culture. His doctoral research explored the role of intersecting identities in gendered environments, and his work has gone on to have a sustainable and systemic impact on government, third sector and higher education across the world.

Review group Sola Adeleke, Ambreen Chohan, Karen Lipsedge, Benita Odogwu-Atkinson, Dionne Spencer, Nkasi Stoll

Acknowledgements

This book would not have been possible without the following people. I would firstly like to thank our critical friends who provided great insight into how best to position this work in the sector, offering kind words of encouragement and support for the role of the book.

I would like to thank the review group for providing critical feedback on chapters prior to submitting to the publisher, and who have been instrumental in challenging the contents of the book to make it the best it can be.

This book would not have been possible if it wasn't for the contributing authors who have shared the most expert rapid reviews of literature and some intimate and painful stories of their experiences of racism across the higher education sector. This expertise and experience that you have all provided will be a stimulus for change.

I thank my partner, Sebastian, who has been standing with me in solidarity with this book, in life, love and my work. I am eternally grateful for you.

I would like to thank my parents and siblings for being encouraging, enthusiastic and engaged in this work, and in tackling race inequalities. I feel that sharing our experiences has brought us closer together and I am incredibly appreciative that we can talk freely and share our frustration about the problem of racism as a family; it helps me continue the work I do.

Preface

In 2019, I had started considering the idea of producing a book that would enable an entire sector to act on tackling racism and intersectional inequalities in higher education. When reflecting on my time in higher education, the triggers for this idea had been bred out of my own personal experiences and professional understanding of interpersonal and institutional racism.

As the editor for the book, I feel it is important for the reader to understand that editing this work has been painful and emotional. It has triggered my own experiences of racial trauma during my time in higher education. When I was a younger gay and Indian undergraduate student, I noticed that none of the Psychology theory I was being taught referenced any evidence or literature from outside North America or Europe, and one module on Cultural Psychology was still somewhat Eurocentric. Outside the classroom, I was subject to racial abuse in the LGBTQI+ community, where I was often called a 'Paki' in the street, and where I was assaulted in a club for sitting on a chair; I was told that chairs were not for people like me. In my life, I have been too Brown to be gay, or too gay to be Brown, and that is a conflict I couldn't accept for a long time and resulted in my experience of mental illness.

During my postgraduate career, I was referred to as 'corner shop' by other students, which they called 'banter'. I felt it was easier to go along with these aggressions to cope. In some ways, I had expected this from other students, as I could rationalise it in my head as being related to alcoholism or a generic immaturity. However, as I delved further into my doctoral research, I learnt that racism was not always so explicit. It sometimes meant being treated differently and unfairly compared with my White peers. During my research career, I was screamed at by a senior academic, a victim of gaslighting from other senior academics and during my first time in Australia at an academic conference, I was actively excluded from being invited to meet with my supervisors' teams, to name a few of many instances. One experience that continues to haunt me was being trapped in an office with two senior academics, who after I had made a rectifiable mistake on a conference presentation by forgetting to include their names under the presenter field, they chastised, humiliated and threatened me across what felt like the longest 30-ish minutes of my life. I wasn't allowed to leave the office, with one senior academic blocking the exit and the other a simple bystander. I had found out that my White colleagues had not experienced this behaviour from these senior academics. It was this experience that silenced me for the rest of my PhD.

These experiences compounded and led me to leave academia. I was forced to leave my dream of one day becoming a professor because the racism I experienced was unbearable. I live with that trauma every day, like so many of my other Black, Asian and minoritised ethnic peers, colleagues and friends. These experiences drove the idea of this action book into becoming reality.

Shortly after reimmersing myself in the works of bell hooks (1990), in particular the book titled *Yearning: Race, Gender, and Cultural Politics*, I revisited a popular quote from hooks, who writes, '[O]ne of the most vital ways we sustain ourselves is by building communities of resistance, places where we know we are not alone' (p 227). Being mindful of this notion of a community of resistance, I hosted two large events and put a call out to my networks, asking for individuals to come together to contribute to this book. I was appreciative, grateful and honoured to be surrounded by individuals and a community of people who have shared great energy and support with each other. Between editing chapters, I have had the honour of speaking with a variety of people who are incredibly passionate about advancing race equality across the sector, who share racial trauma and who are there to support and console each other in times of hardship, marginalisation and adversity. In doing this, we produced a typescript of a full book in less then six months as part of a rapidly forming and acting community of resistance.

Advancing equality, equity and race equality is a cause that for many people stems from their own lived experiences, and to ensure that future generations do not have to experience the adversities we have experienced, I, like many others, have put my vulnerabilities on the line in the hope that society will listen, act and change.

References

hooks, b. (1990) *Yearning: Race, Gender, and Cultural Politics.* New York: South End Press.

PART I

Introduction

1

Positioning anti-racism in higher education

Arun Verma

Anti-Racism in Higher Education: An Action Guide for Change is a direct response to the calls to action and progression in developing and practising anti-racism across the higher education (HE) sector. HE as a sector and universities play a significant role in advancing society, providing opportunities for people and communities to be liberated and successful through education. Universities hold an intrinsic role in local and national communities and play a significant role in bringing diverse talent to different areas of the United Kingdom (UK). The conception of this book came through the collective action with racialised people of colour who continue to live through, witness, see, hear and be exposed to all forms of racism, from covert exclusion to barriers in career progression and through to the widening degree-awarding gap and cultures that prevent university staff and students from being successful and having the same opportunities as their White counterparts in HE.

After a call for interest on social media, Black, Asian and minority ethnic staff and student experts (by their professional and/or personal experiences) were invited to participate in contributing ideas, support and chapters to this action guide to facilitate, critically challenge and enable HE institutions to start a sustainable and authentic anti-racist journey. This book actively and constructively serves to disrupt the HE sector and systems

3

through collective, participatory and intersectional evidence-based issues and solutions. When advocating for constructive disruption, we conceptualise that disruption is simply defined as a break or interruption in a normal course or process. We live in a society where racism is normalised, and any act of calling out race inequalities in different spaces is a form of disruption. To enact disruption requires an understanding of the system in which you are trying to disrupt and the part in which you are looking to interrupt normalised racist praxis. This action guide recognises core parts of the HE system and offers opportunity for transformation and change.

When considering the notion and ideas of constructive disruption, the book acknowledges the colonial and imperial structures that make up HE systems and structures, which play a critical role in the perpetuation of oppression, inequality and inequity within HE. While this book is a direct response and tool to facilitate actions to advance race equality across HE, we are mindful of the wider context and debate in which the work is situated. We recognise the politicisation and sensitivities that come with discourses and narratives pertaining to advancing race equality, and while this book is not the one solution to addressing racial disparities and racism across this sector, the contributions throughout it showcase the opportunities to unlearn, learn and relearn what it means to be engaged and acting upon doing anti-racist work. In order to fully immerse into the book's content, contributions, stories and reflections, we offer some reflections and learning on the power of language, discourses and narratives concerning race equality to help contextualise the different knowledges and schools of thought of each chapter's approach to addressing race inequalities and inequities.

The introduction aims to set the context for the evidence, experiences, questions and recommendations for change across HE. It outlines some of the key narratives and discourses in advancing race equality, while being cognisant of the legacies that have been left by colonial and imperial histories. The lens of intersectionality is a tool to make sense of the ways in which overlapping and simultaneous structures of inequality, oppression and racism is explored and acted upon. Tackling such systems requires agents and majoritised communities to acknowledge such privilege to distribute power and enable racialised and minoritised people to be seen and heard, and to fully participate in a system where they are continuously marginalised and oppressed. The following sections unpack some of the core narratives in the realm and school of anti-racism.

Narratives of race equality

The discourses and narratives of race equality have come under significant debate, with specific questions and sensitivities concerning the use of terms like 'intersectionality' and 'Critical Race Theory', which have often been highlighted as divisive and exclusive in political debate and discussion. Such terms and language have often been used to highlight inequities within the United States of America; however, this book highlights and recontextualises this language within the British HE system. We explore how this language and rhetoric can be used to cultivate and nurture inclusivity while critically reflecting on ways in which systems require intervention and action to facilitate belongingness, fairness and equity, especially within the UK HE system. We also recognise the importance that tackling race inequalities plays, with specific reference to hate speech and widening racial disparities, in addressing broader issues pertaining to society and sustainability (United Nations, 2017). The growing debate and discussion of such language is not novel to the literature and knowledges within race equality work, and this section offers an opportunity to re-establish such terms within the HE system in the UK.

Equality, diversity and inclusion

The mainstreaming of equality, diversity and inclusion, commonly known as EDI, within the HE sector has seen financial and strategic investment in creating EDI teams and leadership posts to support EDI agendas within this sector. EDI teams and strategies are often held within Human Resources (HR) (or People and Culture) departments or divisions within universities. They play a critical role in developing strategic and operational planning and implementation of diversity and inclusion programmes and interventions to support the monitoring and impact across university institutions. With such significant investment in EDI within UK universities, we seek to offer a provocation to reconsider where EDI, as we know it now, came from and what it has evolved to become in modern UK universities.

The Equality Act 2010 came into effect to bring together multiple equality laws, including iterations of the Race Relations Act 1965, under one Act (EHRC, 2021). The impact of this Act was evaluated in 2013, produced by the Centre for Research in Social Policy and the International Centre for Public and Social Policy on behalf of the Government Equalities Office (Equally Ours, 2021). Equality, diversity and inclusion are brought together to illustrate the theme and function of the team(s) and role(s) within an organisation. Equality, within HE systems, speaks to enable equitable fairness and equal opportunity to all individuals within the HE institution to access, participate and bring about their success. Diversity can be described as identifying opportunities, approaches and interventions that celebrate and increase diversity across HE institutions and organisations (Roberson, 2006). Inclusion refers to a core outcome for equality/equity, diversity and inclusion (EEDI) teams, to focus on working towards an environment and culture in which all communities within HE can thrive, feel belonging and be included to enable their retention and success within and beyond the walls of HE (Roberson, 2006).

With a legislative framework in place that outlines and protects characteristics of racially and minoritised groups, organisations have a legal obligation to demonstrate and act upon protecting racialised and minoritised communities from discrimination, abuse and harm in society and organisations (EHRC, 2021). Evidence like the McKinsey & Company 'Why Diversity Matters' report (2015) began to highlight the clear benefits of embracing diversity in organisations that enable institutions and organisations to enhance their success, growth and impact. Increasing evidence and mainstreaming of EEDI can be seen to be further embedded into strategies highlighting the importance of EEDI roles, teams, organisation, education and learning in organisations (for example, Sharples, 2019). However, it is important to note that EEDI functions have typically been positioned in HR departments in organisations, due to the proximity to monitoring and evaluating employee recruitment, retention and success data within these companies (Barron, 2019). Recent years have seen EEDI teams and roles start to serve beyond the realms and confines of HR, as we see organisations rethinking EEDI beyond employee and recruitment data through to an organisation's products, partnerships and services too (Barron, 2019). There is some debate concerning the role of anti-racism within EDI spaces. We can pose some questions as to whether the modern role and function of EEDI is suited to anti-racism work. In what ways does racism get lost in the broader world of EEDI and how might we centre tackling racism among a culture of competing inequalities? Some of these questions are addressed throughout this book, and each contributing author provides a critical view on addressing the crisis of racism.

Racism

Mike Cole (2017) wrote 'if race is a social construct, racism is a frighteningly real, burning and omnipresent issue. It is directed at people because of a number of perceived identities: race, ethnicity, nationality, religion or a combination of these.' Racism by a reductionist definition is considered the abuse, discrimination and prejudice of groups of people according to their racial and/or ethnic group (Wodak and Reisigl, 2015). In an analysis of the etymological discourses of racism, Wodak and Reisigl found that practices and processes that perpetuate racism are premised on the marking of cultural differences and polarisation in constructing larger and more homogenous groups (for example, Black, Asian and minority ethnic), and that this embedding of race as a social construction is 'accompanied by the hierarchization and negative evaluation of the racialised Other' (2015, pp 578–9). This book is written noting that racism is a part of our cultural and societal fabric, and it continues to marginalise and oppress racialised Black, Asian and minority ethnic communities in the UK through a multiplicity of modes and complexities (for example, Phillips et al, 2020).

When unpacking and reconceptualising racism for this book, authors refer to different domains of racism, more commonly distinguished as structural or institutional racism (Lander, 2021). The term institutional racism gained attention after the traumatic handling and tragic death of Stephen Lawrence (Lea, 2000). This murder was followed by a report led by MacPherson (1999), providing clarity on this term as noted by Dr Benjamin Bowling, stating that

> institutional racism is the process by which people from ethnic minorities are systematically discriminated against by a range of public and private bodies. If the result or outcome of established laws, customs or practices is racially discriminatory, then institutional racism can be said to have occurred. Although racism is rooted in widely shared attitudes, values and beliefs, discrimination can occur irrespective of the intent of the individuals who carry out the activities of the institution.

Although this quote speaks to institutions like that of policing, education and others, it frames racism in an institutional context, where organised structures and processes enable and perpetuate racism. When considering institutional racism within HE, despite equalities legislation, racism manifests in hidden or covert forms through Black, Asian and minoritised ethnic people's silencing, exclusion from decision making, cultural insensitivities and racial aggressions (Bhopal and Henderson, 2021). In accordance with UK law, perpetrators of racial abuse and harassment are committing a hate crime; however, such crimes are not often held to account and seen through in institutions (Laverick and Joyce, 2020). It is important to note the role of 'everyday racism', commonly referred to as microaggressions (Williams, 2021), which are often considered harmless by majoritised groups, which is defined thus: 'everyday racism is racism, but not all racism is everyday racism. From everyday racism there is no relief' (p 202). 'Consequently, microaggressions and everyday discrimination have been linked to numerous mental health problems as well as physical health problems and poor quality of life' (Williams, 2020, as cited in Williams, 2021, pp 880–81). Examples are commonly rising to the surface, with some higher education institutions (HEIs) listing examples of microaggressions on their EDI web pages (for example, University of Edinburgh, 2021). These aggressions may also take the form of racial gaslighting, which is described by Johnson et al (2020, p 1029) as a

> particularly common and harmful type of victim blaming … the definition of gaslighting can be extended to include a single act or series of acts perpetrated by any person in a position of power designed to manipulate less powerful others to doubt themselves or question their own sanity or memory (Davis and Ernst, 2019; Tobias and Joseph, 2020). … Gaslighting is used not only to maintain or gain power in intimate relationships but also to uphold power structures of White supremacy, patriarchy, heteronormativity, and transphobia [and] applies to interactions between cis- and transgender people, heterosexual people and LGBTQIA+ people, and Whites and people of color.

Contributing authors within this book discuss examples and experiences of microaggressions, and we further argue that there is nothing 'micro' about aggression, and these are simply aggressive acts of racism, or 'racial aggression(s)', which result in trauma.

Structural racism speaks to the ways in which political and societal processes are embedded with values, behaviours and attitudes that critically contribute to the marginalisation and racialisation of Black, Asian and minority ethnic communities (Hussain, 2021). Racial disparities and inequity can be seen in outcomes for Black, Asian and minority ethnic people across different institutions (Arday, 2021). For example, Otu et al (2020) highlight the impact of structural racism in the realm of health inequalities, noting 'that COVID-19 was more likely to be diagnosed among Black ethnic groups compared to White ethnic groups with the highest mortality occurring among Black, Asian and minority ethnic persons and persons living in the more deprived areas' (n.p.). Further intersectional disparities are highlighted in the health systems, where Black and/or Asian women are recorded to have a higher maternal mortality rate, which is a disparity further exacerbated when factoring in deprivation and socioeconomic status (Knight et al, 2020). When looking at education and considerations of structural racism, there are clear disparities in the degree-awarding gap between Black, Asian and minority ethnic people and White people (Jones et al, n.d.). This is shown in data where 25 per cent more of a White student cohort achieved a first- or upper-second-class degree than the Black, Asian and minority ethnic cohort (McDuff et al, 2018), and it has been noted that ethnic minority graduates from Russell Group universities are less likely to succeed in the labour market and often undertake further graduate education to avoid and deter unemployment (Lessard-Phillips et al, 2018).

The role of structural and institutional racism across society and specifically in HE pervade and perpetuate the marginalisation and deprivation of Black, Asian and minority ethnic people in terms of their life chances, wellbeing and outcomes in society (also noted by Lander, 2021). Throughout this book, authors make references to the interplay of both structural and institutional racism in relation to their expertise and experience, where suggested changes are noted to support the transforming of structures and institutions in the drive towards anti-racism.

Anti-racism

The term anti-racism has gained a great deal of traction over recent years, as there has been a shift from the bystander position of 'not being racist' to playing a more active role in changing systems to enable positive outcomes for Black, Asian and minority ethnic people (Miller, 2021). John Amaechi (2020, n.p.) notes that:

> Anti-racists are different, and they come in all shapes and sizes. They come in all ages. Anti-racists are constantly looking around to say, what tools do I have available to make it clear that this is not acceptable? And this, this is what anti-racists do. It's not that they stand up at the dinner table when their uncle's a little

bit racist and kick the turkey off. That's not it. But what they do is they say, I'm sorry uncle John. That's not acceptable. That's racist. Quietly and respectfully. What they do is they make sure that they never miss an opportunity to let the world know where they stand, even if they can't change everything.

While this argument positions the role of being an anti-racist, there has been a significant evolution of anti-racism throughout history, thought and activism (Bhattacharyya et al, 2020). Anti-racism has continued to be a movement of those who are subject to the structural and hierarchical power of racism recognising the shared experience of racism and forming collective action to oppose it in the many ways it manifests itself (Meer, 2019). Anti-racism is rooted as collective action against racism, and stems from a reaction to the marginalisation and oppression of enslaved Black communities, through colonialism and imperialism, which have contributed to an 'ontological imprint both in how it [colonialism and imperialism] constructed a particular anti-blackness and a kind of dehumanisation of the black body that Wilderson III describes as "social death"' (Aouragh, 2019, p 9). When looking back through history, individual experiences were a stimulus in generating mass and collective action; however, such leaders of movements and anti-racism resistance have almost always ended in their demise and have often become hidden figures in history (Aouragh, 2019). This is also characterised as 'strategic silence', which refers to the intersectional suppression of minoritised and racialised groups (Müller, 2021).

Recent applications of anti-racism becoming mainstreamed across HE institutions have been producing and sharing an anti-racism action plan (for example, UAL, 2021), and even more broadly the European Union have launched an Anti-Racism Action Plan for 2020–2025 (Müller, 2021), indicating a bold ambition to achieve anti-racism. However, such development of actions plans can often neglect the critical challenges to inclusive improvement and implementation (Ladhani and Sitter, 2020). This book supports the reader in immersing themself into the challenge and identify sustainable and transformational actions. It is important to note that the work of anti-racism can accelerate wider EEDI strategy, policy and programmes, and is not an exclusive or siloed approach to EEDI (Perue et al, 2021). The mainstreaming of an anti-racism narrative and movement through institutional and structural systems has the caveat that universalising anti-racism dilutes its history and power as a movement against racism (Seikkula, 2019).

Intersectionality

The term intersectionality was born out of the school of thought concerning critical theory from the voices and expertise of Black feminist scholars (for example, Crenshaw, 1989). It derives from a school of thought which notes that the concept of race is not rooted in biology but is socially constructed in a form that continues to minoritise and racialise people of colour (Delgado and Stefancic, 2017). It was brought into light by Kimberlé Crenshaw in her 1989 paper titled 'Mapping the Margins'. It was in this article that Crenshaw discussed intersectionality in three parts: structural, political and representational. Structural intersectionality refers to the positioning of marginalised people at intersections of multiple racialised and/or minoritised identities. Considerations of political intersectionality explore the wider policies and political rhetoric that perpetuate the marginalisation of racialised and/or minoritised communities. In Crenshaw's paper, she also refers to representational intersectionality, explaining the role of societal and cultural images and language that continue the marginalisation of racialised and minoritised people.

The role of intersectionality is crucial to the advancement of race and intersectional equality and embedding anti-racism into policy and praxis. Tools including the intersectionality wheel have surfaced to enable organisations to diligently integrate intersectionality into research, EDI spaces, programmes, products and services (Simpson, 2009). Such guidance and toolkits have been developed to aid teams to move beyond disaggregating staff and/or student data to examine how the qualitative experiences of the marginalised and racialised groups reflect and act on tackling structural inequalities. The role of intersectionality serves as a holistic bridge that connects the complexity of experiences in the positioning of structures, identities, praxis, histories and systems that enable inequalities. Through the book, the chapters draw on intersectional experiences to reflect and bring to life the intersecting inequalities that exist and are perpetuated within different parts of the HE institution.

Colonialism and imperialism

When considering the systematic construction and oppression of people racialised as Black, Asian and minority ethnic, these can be rooted in the impact of colonial and imperial power and exploitation (Blakemore, 2019). Despite colonialism and imperialism being used synonymously, there is a clear distinction between the two issues. Colonialism can be described as 'the control by individuals or groups over territory and/or behaviour of other individuals or groups ... seen as a form of exploitation with emphasis on economic variables ... and as a culture change process ... [through] the idea of domination' (Horvarth, 1972, p 46). Imperialism is a result of empires, and through discussion in a paper exploring multiple lenses of imperialism, it has been characterised through many definitions including

> the process or policy of establishing or maintaining an empire ... the ruthless drive for dominance ... threatening peace abroad and freedom at home ... [the] standard term of abuse, mostly applied to Western powers, including the United States. Here it [is] often conjoined with "colonialism" as a kind of synonym, though increasingly colonialism supplanted imperialism. (Kumar, 2021, p 285–6)

Throughout history, European and Western forces have justified their power dominance through the assertion of non-European/Western and predominantly non-White countries being cast as 'savage' or 'barbaric' nations (Blakemore, 2019). The legacy of colonial and imperial oppression has led to 'environmental degradation, the spread of disease, economic instability, ethnic rivalries, and human rights violations' (Blakemore, 2019). These legacies have created intergenerational trauma resulting in the 'discharge signals that emanate from the trauma of slavery [preventing] individuals from crying or raging about the oppression of racism' (Mariska, Habibi & Farisi, 2019, p 118), and in effect a silencing of the global majority.

When considering the role of Britishness, there has been considerable analysis of colonial racism within British politics in light of Brexit (Virdee & McGeever, 2018). Virdee and McGeever highlight that the role of colonial racism has had a systemic impact on English nationalism where 'racism has become normalised in both elite political discourses and practice and everyday life, dramatically diminishing the spaces for Britain's racialised minorities to breath and live life free from hate' (p 1811). The impact of colonialism and imperialism is perpetuated across the British HE system as an approach to renewing the UK's imperialist legacy of power (Boussebaa, 2020). Doku (2019) commented on how UK universities and the academic circles were instrumental in the justification, perpetuation and preservation of the British Empire. Doku further comments that such colonial legacies have perpetuated marginalisation and oppression of Black people and their contribution to knowledge and scholarship. This can be seen in racial disparities concerning attainment and award gaps with a 'clear hangover from a time when White European scholarship was explicitly viewed as superior to all else. While external factors play their role, a significant body of evidence shows that the Academy reinforces rather than works against the wider structural inequalities' (n.p.).

Movements that aim to decolonise the curriculum seek to dismantle the adverse legacies of colonialism and imperialism within HE (Felix, 2019), and examples of this can be seen through the work of campaigns and programmes including 'Why is my curriculum White?' (Begum & Saini, 2019) and the Decolonising DMU (2021). In 2021, the Higher Education Policy Institute (HEPI) published a report exploring perspectives on decolonising the curriculum, highlighting that 'people are largely hostile or in two minds about "decolonising" the curriculum. ... Yet, when asked about broadening the curriculum to take in people, events, materials and subjects from across the world, 67%

approve – with just 4% against' (2021, n.p.). The evidence from HEPI highlights disparities in views, and while the report calls for thoughtfulness in implementing decolonisation, there is a critical element in supporting more people to build confidence with an understanding of the connections between decolonisation, diversity and inclusion work, what it is and what it aims to do. Decolonisation is an opportunity to eliminate racism and inequalities from pedagogy, teaching and learning while adding to societal histories, identities, structures and cultures that move towards a more independent and intersectional curriculum (a detailed conceptualisation of this can be found in Shain et al, 2021). Undoing colonialism is about undoing the processes and practices that perpetuate inequalities (for example, Ndlovu-Gatsheni, 2019). This book refers to the varying adversities and longstanding impact of colonialism and imperialism on all parts of the HE system, with authors referencing the role of decolonising universities, particularly within the pedagogies of HE teaching, learning, scholarship and research. This is in sections of the book where authors speak to the work of decolonisation to remove racism and inequality from the curriculum, while adding to histories to enable and enrich the HE curriculum.

Privilege, power and fragility

It is through colonial and imperial legacy that Whiteness has maintained its supremacy, power and privilege across the UK, Europe and the West. Sara Ahmed (2007) conceptualises Whiteness not as a racial identity but 'described as an ongoing and unfinished history, which orientates bodies in specific directions, affecting how they "take up" space ... that Whiteness is an orientation that puts certain things within reach' (p 150). Ahmed explores the positioning of Whiteness through the lens of phenomenology, highlighting how bodies are influenced by the histories and legacies of colonialism. These legacies have served to Whiten the world and make it ready for White people and bodies to occupy it (Fanon, 1986). In 1988, Peggy McIntosh wrote about 'White privilege' through the metaphor of the invisible knapsack. Through her autobiographical account McIntosh (1988, n.p.), she wrote,

I had come to see White privilege as an invisible package of unearned assets that I could count on cashing in each day but about which I was meant to remain oblivious. White privilege is like an invisible, weightless knapsack of special provisions, maps, passports, code books, visas, clothes, tools, and blank checks. Seeing this, which I was taught not to see, made me revise my view of myself, and also of the United States' claim to be a democracy in which merit is rewarded and life outcomes are directly related to deservedness.

Gillborn (2006) refers to making sense of White privilege through the lens of power and supremacy, also referred to as White supremacy. In his article 'Rethinking White Supremacy' (p 320), he highlights that

White supremacy is not only, nor indeed primarily, associated with relatively small and extreme political movements that openly mobilize on the basis of race hatred (important and dangerous though such groups are): rather, supremacy is seen to relate to the operation of forces that saturate the everyday, mundane actions and policies that shape the world in the interests of White people.

It is through a framing of a 'Whiteworld' that Gillborn articulates society and spaces that White people take for granted, while those racialised as non-White groups experience otherness and oppression. McIntosh (1988) raises awareness of White privilege, with a view to enabling recognition of those with power to acknowledge that privileging systems pervade society and distribute power to effect inclusion and change.

Despite the values of and the assertion that White privilege is a tool to dismantle racism and distribute power to the most marginalised and oppressed in society, this can often be met by fragility (Murdoch & McAloney-Kocaman, 2019). When White privilege is called out in systems and society, it is met with fragility when 'majority group members experience stress as a consequence of challenges to the racial status quo and result in the activation of greater prejudice and discrimination towards the minority group as a defensive mechanism' (p 205), with examples of White individuals reporting more personal hardship to distance themselves from 'privilege' (Murdoch & McAloney-Kocaman, 2019). In a study by Murdoch and McAloney-Kocaman, they found that White majority people were 'claiming more life hardships [to] serve to help deny the presence of White privilege in one's personal life, despite life hardships not being relevant to White privilege as a general construct' (p 209). This denial of privilege can be seen as an exception to the privileged majority, but still reaping the benefits of being elevated within the racial hierarchy.

Throughout this book the contributors share provocative questions that enable the reader to reconsider the acknowledgement of their privileges and the ways in which these can be utilised to distribute power to the most marginalised and deprived in society.

Why this guide?

The book offers an action stance on existing literature and evidence to advancing race equality within the HE sphere. It serves to be functional and supportive to those who are driving EEDI policy, strategy, programmes and interventions, and to enable those not familiar with anti-racism to critically learn, reflect and act. It enables these groups to approach change through a systems and implementation lens and framework. The guide was produced with intersectionality at its heart, and it intertwines the voices and expertise of Black, Asian and minority ethnic staff and students from across a variety of racial, cultural and ethnic backgrounds, genders, classes and disabilities to showcase the power of participation, collective voice, effort and action in driving changes towards anti-racism in HE. The book offers an opportunity for the HE sector to demystify language associated with race equality, and for it be framed within the context of inclusion, dignity, compassion and respect.

The structure of the guide and its respective chapters have been curated and built up with a typical HE institutional system in mind, pertaining to staff, students, research, teaching, pedagogy, governance, operations and strategy. This guide serves to reflect core parts of HE institutions and offer critical guidance and reflection on how these systems continue to perpetuate racism and at what points change can happen to dismantle racism in the institution. It provides an intimate space for the reader to immerse themself into different parts of the HE system through the lenses of racism, intersectionality, privilege, power, equality and inclusion, and strives to facilitate a space and opportunity for learning and development and to conspire with, enable and empower racialised and minoritised people.

Audience

This book is written to all those interested and involved in HE to participate in becoming anti-racist as individuals, communities and institutions. As a society, advancing race equality requires everyone's involvement and action and there is an opportunity for those to explore and discover racial issues in this book. For students, we recognise students' unions and associations playing a critical role in race equality, and encourage student representatives, presidents and vice-presidents to immerse themselves in the book to consider and develop opportunities to act on change with their associated university. We encourage Black, Asian and minority ethnic staff and student networks to use this guide to empower networks to change and hold their institutions to account for driving and building anti-racist cultures. There are many staff involved in leading EDI initiatives both through academic and professional services work, and we encourage those who have significant EDI leadership roles to utilise this book to inform, support and sustain the work they are doing through a systems, impact and implementation framework, which is interwoven in the book.

Format of the guide

The book offers functionality and proactiveness as its core values, while recognising the evidence that underpins the issues in some detail. It combines evidence with a focus on sharing the voice of racialised and minoritised communities, the areas for change as recommended by contributors' analysis and insights, along with critical questions posed to the reader to nurture and sustain changes to thinking about what it means to become anti-racist in a HE institution. Each chapter uses a similar formula to ensure consistency and enable the reader to utilise this book in different ways, which could be in learning, strategy development, implementation and generating innovation in the realm of anti-racism.

Rapid review

Each chapter presents a summary of the dominant themes and issues pertinent to the area of interest across academic and non-academic literature from 2010 onwards, while ensuring highly cited and critical literature prior to 2010 is also referenced. While the rapid evidence reviews vary in size throughout the book, it is important to recognise that the literature cited in this book is not exhaustive. The editor recognises and acknowledges the range of literature, scholarship and research that has been conducted over time. Contributors have referenced a range of literature from academic journals and books through to public articles, newspapers and opinion pieces. The purpose of doing this is to ensure that the reader has a clear idea of the existence of evidence and literature in this area. We encourage the reader to utilise the references in each section of the book to help further their understanding and knowledge in a particular part of the HE system in practising anti-racism. While some of these sections throughout the book are written in brief, they provide an opportunity for those reading to reconsider the existing evidence in an action form, while also being signposted to instrumental contributions to the knowledge of advancing race equality in HE and beyond.

Voice and empowerment

This section includes a narrative from published articles and/or a personal account of an author's or peer's experiences of racism in relation to the chapter and sub-chapter's theme. The inclusion of this section was an opportunity for authors to write their experiences, thoughts, feelings and emotions in relation to the chapter's theme. This reflects the core value of intersectionality in centring the voice of racialised and minoritised people (Hernández, 2005). It is an opportunity for the reader to see how the issues and themes presented in evidence come to life through the stories of those racialised as Black, Asian and/or minority ethnic.

Change domains

The focus in this book is on facilitating and nurturing sustainable and implementable actions to advance race equality. These actions and interventions are designed to evoke change in a system that perpetuates racism (Creegan et al, 2003). Change can be simply conceptualised as making something different, modifying and amending something. Change can be considered in the form of a prism representing different facets and directions, with a focus on the cultural (a common set of ideas, values, attitudes and behaviours common to a group and region) and time (the ways in which organisational structures, processes, policy and practice shift and adjust in relation to the outputs that have been achieved (Varnum & Grossmann, 2017). When referring to cultural change Varnum and Grossmann write that 'the notion of change on the cultural scale likely also concerns a multitude of factors, including evolution of ideas, refinement of practices, reactions to shifts in social-ecological affordances, and so on' (p 2). This notion of change embraces complexity, recognising that this change results in the evolution of society; however, the direction of evolution is dependent on the kind of actions and interventions that can steer its direction (Rogers, 2017).

As noted earlier in the introduction, advancing race equality requires change. Initiating and sustaining intersectional change are areas of complexity when done in partnership with racialised and minoritised communities and implemented considering the influence of social policy, political rhetoric and environments (Stanley et al, 2019; Allen et al, 2021). Domains of change offer up critical points within the HE sub-system where an intervention can instigate and embed a change into the heart of the system (for example, Atkins et al, 2017). The change domains presented by contributors throughout this book are targeted areas generated from the rapid evidence review and narrative that professional and personal experts of racism have highlighted for change, intervention and further investigation within HE institutions and across the sector. The change domains presented are not prescriptive to all HE institutions, and the reader may need to consider ways in which such domains can be adapted and incorporated into different and unique institutional contexts and systems.

Reflective questions

The role of reflection and dialogue is central to the function and culture of EDI in the HE system (Atewologun & Mahalingam, 2018). In order to consider opportunities for change, people within institutions need to recognise that EDI is not solely a workplace issue but transcends between intersecting personal and professional identities across space, place and time (Verma, 2020). Questions in the form posed throughout this book can be conceptualised as rhetorical in nature, where some questions do not necessarily require an answer or response, questions are posed to assert a critical race issue in British society and HE, and/ or such questions may be responded to depending on how the reader makes sense of the question (Biezma & Rawlins, 2017).

The questions offered here are presented to nurture constructively disruptive conversations about racism in their institutions related to the theme. It is an opportunity for groups and committees across the sector to critically reflect on questions to help create learning opportunities to advance race equality and move towards anti-racism.

Contributions and authorship

The book itself is comprised of multiple submissions from experts from personal and/or professional lived and subject expertise in race equality, and wider diversity and inclusion work within and beyond HE. When reading each chapter, we encourage readers to appreciate that each named contributing author has provided diligent provocations, learning and reflection for the reader's consideration. We also take this opportunity to challenge the inequalities that come with authorship and authorship order in academic research (for example, Hart & Perlis, 2021; Myers et al, 2021; Panter, 2021). This book challenges traditionally archaic, racist and patriarchal inequalities concerning authorship and authorship order (Chakravartty et al, 2018), and strongly encourages the reader to recognise and reference sections and chapters, acknowledging all the authors' expert contributions across each section you read. When citing chapters and respective sections, we invite the reader to explicitly acknowledge the contributions of all authors where possible and to reconsider approaches to more inclusive authorship and knowledge production that enables equity and empowerment for those less heard and seen in HE and academic teaching, scholarship and research (Chakravartty et al, 2018).

References

Ahmed, S. (2007) A phenomenology of whiteness. *Feminist Theory*, 8(2), 149–68.

Allen, K., Cuthbert, K., Hall, J. J., Hines, S. & Elley, S. (2021) Trailblazing the gender revolution? Young people's understandings of gender diversity through generation and social change. *Journal of Youth Studies*, DOI: 10.1080/ 13676261.2021.1923674.

Amaechi, J. (2020) Not-racist v anti-racist: what's the difference? Accessed 7 July 2021, from www.bbc.co.uk/bitesize/articles/ zs9n2v4

Aouragh, M. (2019) 'White privilege' and shortcuts to anti-racism. *Race & Class*, 61(2), 3–26.

Arday, J. (2021) Race, education, and social mobility: we all need to dream the same dream and want the same thing. *Educational Philosophy and Theory*, 53(3), 227–32, DOI: 10.1080/ 00131857.2020.1777642.

Atewologun, D. & Mahalingam, R. (2018) Intersectionality as a methodological tool in qualitative equality, diversity and inclusion research. In *Handbook of Research Methods in Diversity Management, Equality and Inclusion at Work*. Cheltenham: Edward Elgar Publishing.

Atkins, L., Francis, J., Islam, R., O'Connor, D., Patey, A., Ivers, N. Foy, R., Duncan, E. M., Colquhoun, H., Grimshaw, J. M., Lawton, R. & Michie, S. (2017) A guide to using the Theoretical Domains Framework of behaviour change to investigate implementation problems. *Implementation Science*, 12(1), 1–18.

Barron, D. (2019) Who has responsibility for D&I? Accessed 2 July 2021, from www.irishtimes.com/special-reports/diversity-inclusion/who-has-responsibility-for-d-i-1.4052428

Begum, N. & Saini, R. (2019) Decolonising the curriculum. *Political Studies Review*, 17(2), 196–201.

Bhattacharyya, G., Virdee, S. & Winter, A. (2020) Revisiting histories of anti-racist thought and activism. *Identities*, 27(1), 1–19.

Bhopal, K. & Henderson, H. (2021) Competing inequalities: gender versus race in higher education institutions in the UK. *Educational Review*, 73(2), 153–69.

Biezma, M. & Rawlins, K. (2017) Rhetorical questions: severing asking from questioning. *Semantics and Linguistic Theory*, 27, 302–22.

Blakemore, E. (2019) Colonialism facts and information. Accessed 11 July 2021, from www.nationalgeographic.com/culture/article/colonialism

Boussebaa, M. (2020) In the shadow of empire: global Britain and the UK business school. *Organization*, 27(3), 483–93.

Chakravartty, P., Kuo, R., Grubbs, V. & McIlwain, C. (2018) #CommunicationSoWhite. *Journal of Communication*, 68(2), 254–66.

Cole, M. (2017) Racism in the UK: continuity and change. In *Education, Equality and Human Rights*, (pp 52–98). London: Routledge.

Creegan, C., Colgan, F., Charlesworth, R. & Robinson, G. (2003) Race equality policies at work: employee perceptions of the 'implementation gap' in a UK local authority. *Work, Employment and Society*, 17(4), 617–40.

Crenshaw, K. (1989) Mapping the margins: intersectionality, identity politics, and violence against women of color. *Stan. L. Rev.*, 43, 1241.

Davis, A. M. & Ernst, R. (2019) Racial gaslighting. *Politics, Groups, and Identities*, 7(4), 761–74. DOI: 10.1080/21565503.2017.1403934.

De Montfort University (DMU). (2021) Decolonising DMU. Accessed 11 July 2021, from https://decolonisingdmu.our.dmu.ac.uk/

Delgado, R. & Stefancic, J. (2017) *Critical Race Theory*. New York: New York University Press.

Doku, A. (2019) Recognising British colonialism and advancing the Academy. Advance HE. Accessed 8 January 2022, from www.advance-he.ac.uk/news-and-views/Recognising-British-colonialism-and-advancing-the-Academy

Equality and Human Rights Commission (2021) Equality Act 2010. Accessed 2 July 2021, from www.equalityhumanrights.com/en/equality-act/equality-act-2010

Equally Ours (2021) Evaluation of the impact of the Equality Act 2010. Accessed 2 July 2021, from www.equallyours.org.uk/evaluation-of-the-impact-of-the-equality-act-2010

Fanon, F. (1986) *Black Skin, White Masks*. London: Pluto Press.

Felix, M. (2019) To decolonise the curriculum, we have to decolonise ourselves. Accessed 11 July 2021, from https://wonkhe.com/blogs/to-decolonise-the-curriculum-we-have-to-decolonise-ourselves/

Gillborn, D. (2006) 'Rethinking white supremacy: who counts in 'whiteworld'. *Ethnicities*, 6(3), 318–40. DOI: 10.1177/1468796806068323.

Hart, K. L. & Perlis, R. H. (2021) Authorship inequality: a bibliometric study of the concentration of authorship among a diminishing number of individuals in high-impact medical journals, 2008–2019. *BMJ Open*, 11(1). DOI: 10.1136/bmjopen-2020–046002.

HEPI (2021) Views on decolonising the curriculum depend on how changes are presented – HEPI. Accessed 20 November 2021, from www.hepi.ac.uk/2021/07/20/views-on-decolonising-the-curriculum-depend-on-how-changes-are-presented/

Hernández, T. K. (2005) The intersectionality of lived experience and anti-discrimination empirical research. In *Handbook of Employment Discrimination Research* (pp 325–335). Dordrecht: Springer.

Hirschhorn, L. R., Magge, H. & Kiflie, A. (2021) Aiming beyond equality to reach equity: the promise and challenge of quality improvement. *BMJ*, 374. DOI: 10.1136/bmj.n939.

Horvath, R. J. (1972) A definition of colonialism. *Current Anthropology*, 13(1), 45–57.

Hussain, R. (2021) Shining a spotlight on structural racism in Britain today. Accessed 1 August 2021, from www.tuc.org.uk/blogs/shining-spotlight-structural-racism-britain-today

Johnson, V. E., Nadal, K. L., Sissoko, D. R. G. & King, R. (2021) 'It's not in your head': gaslighting, 'splaining, victim blaming, and other harmful reactions to microaggressions. *Perspectives on Psychological Science*, 16(5), 1024–36. DOI: 10.1177/17456916211011963.

Jones, R., Pietersen, A., Amirthalingam, A. & Chizari, M. (n.d.) A collaborative reflection on Black, Asian and minority ethnic (BAME) attainment in higher education. Not yet published.

Knight, M., Bunch, K., Kenyon, S., Tuffnell, D. & Kurinczuk, J. J. (2020) A national population-based cohort study to investigate inequalities in maternal mortality in the United Kingdom, 2009–17. *Paediatric and Perinatal Epidemiology*, 34(4), 392–8.

Kumar, K. (2021) Colony and empire, colonialism and imperialism: a meaningful distinction?. *Comparative Studies in Society and History*, 63(2), 280–309.

Ladhani, S. & Sitter, K. C. (2020) The revival of anti-racism. *Critical Social Work*, 21(1), 54–65.

Lander, V. (2021) Structural racism: what it is and how it works. Accessed 1 August 2021, from https://theconversation.com/structural-racism-what-it-is-and-how-it-works-158822

Laverick, W. & Joyce, N. P. (2020) Reinterpreting the UK response to hate crime. *British Journal of Community Justice*, 16(1), 82–102.

Lea, J. (2000) The Macpherson Report and the question of institutional racism. *The Howard Journal of Criminal Justice*, 39(3), 219–33.

Lessard-Phillips, L., Boliver, V., Pampaka, M. & Swain, D. (2018) Exploring ethnic differences in the post-university destinations of Russell Group graduates. *Ethnicities*, 18(4), 496–517.

MacPherson, W. (1999) The Stephen Lawrence Inquiry. United Kingdom: The Stationary Office. Accessed 14 November 2021, from http://webarchive.nationalarchives.gov.uk/20130814142233/http://www.archive.official-documents.co.uk/document/cm42/4262/4262.html

Mariska, P. N., Habibi, H. & Farisi, A. B. (2019) Cultural identity of colonialism: traumatic effects of slavery and racism. *Cultura Interpreta*, 9(3), 117–24.

McDuff, N., Tatam, J., Beacock, O. & Ross, F. (2018) Closing the attainment gap for students from black and minority ethnic backgrounds through institutional change. *Widening Participation and Lifelong Learning*, 20(1), 79–101.

McIntosh, P. (1988) Unpacking the invisible knapsack. *Gender Through the Prism of Difference*, 235–8.

McKinsey & Company (2015) Why diversity matters. Accessed 2 July 2021, from www.mckinsey.com/business-functions/organization/our-insights/why-diversity-matters#

Meer, N. (2019) WEB Du Bois, double consciousness and the 'spirit' of recognition. *The Sociological Review*, 67(1), 47–62.

Miller, P. (2021) 'System conditions', system failure, structural racism and anti-racism in the United Kingdom: evidence from education and beyond. *Societies*, 11(2), 42.

Müller, C. (2021) Anti-racism in Europe: an intersectional approach to the discourse on empowerment through the EU Anti-Racism Action Plan 2020–2025. *Social Sciences*, 10(4), 137.

Murdoch, A. & McAloney-Kocaman, K. (2019) Exposure to evidence of white privilege and perceptions of hardships among White UK residents. *Race and Social Problems*, 11(3), 205–11.

Myers, J. S., Lane-Fall, M. & Soong, C. (2021) No one left behind: a case for more inclusivity in authorship for quality improvement and implementation research. *BMJ Quality and Safety*, 30(10), 779–81.

Ndlovu-Gatsheni, S. J. (2019) Provisional notes on decolonizing research methodology and undoing its dirty history. *Journal of Developing Societies*, 35(4), 481–92.

Otu, A., Ahinkorah, B. O., Ameyaw, E. K., Seidu, A. A. & Yaya, S. (2020) One country, two crises: what Covid-19 reveals about health inequalities among BAME communities in the United Kingdom and the sustainability of its health system. *International Journal for Equity in Health*, 19(1), 1–6.

Panter, M. (2021) The ethics of manuscript authorship: best practices for attribution. Accessed 14 November 2021, from www.aje.com/arc/ethics-manuscript-authorship/

Perue, G. L. G., Fox-Rosellini, S. E., Sur, N. B., Marulanda-Londono, E., Margolesky, J., Tornes, L., Bure, A., Kalika, P., Chileuitt, A., Allespach, H., Uthman, B., Alkhachroum, A., Sacco, R. & Monteith, T. S. (2021) Development of an equity, diversity, inclusion, and anti-racism pledge as the foundation for action in an academic department of neurology. *Neurology*, 97(15), 729–36.

Phillips, C., Earle, R., Parmar, A. & Smith, D. (2020) Dear British criminology: where has all the race and racism gone?. *Theoretical Criminology*, 24(3), 427–46.

Roberson, Q. M. (2006) Disentangling the meanings of diversity and inclusion in organizations. *Group & Organization Management*, 31(2), 212–36.

Rogers, J. D. (2017) Dynamic trajectories, adaptive cycles, and complexity in culture change. *Journal of Archaeological Method and Theory*, 24(4), 1326–55.

Seikkula, M. (2019) Adapting to post-racialism? Definitions of racism in non-governmental organization advocacy that mainstreams anti-racism. *European Journal of Cultural Studies*, 22(1), 95–109.

Shain, F., Yıldız, Ü. K., Poku, V. & Gokay, B. (2021) From silence to 'strategic advancement': institutional responses to 'decolonising' in higher education in England. *Teaching in Higher Education*, 26(7–8), 920–36.

Sharples, S. (2019) Leading an EDI strategy in a UK University: reflections from an HFE Professional. In *Advancing Diversity, Inclusion, and Social Justice through Human Systems Engineering* (pp 241–46). Boca Raton: CRC Press.

Simpson, J. (2009) *Everyone Belongs: A Toolkit for Applying Intersectionality*. Ontario: CRIAW.

Stanley, C. A., Watson, K. L., Reyes, J. M. & Varela, K. S. (2019) Organizational change and the chief diversity officer: a case study of institutionalizing a diversity plan. *Journal of Diversity in Higher Education*, 12(3), 255.

Tobias, H. & Joseph, A. (2020) Sustaining systemic racism through psychological gaslighting: Denials of racial profiling and justifications of carding by police utilizing local news media. *Race and Justice*, 10(4), 424–55.

UAL (2021) Anti-racism action plan. Accessed 7 July 2021, from www.arts.ac.uk/__data/assets/pdf_file/0044/288998/UAL-Anti-Racism-Action-Plan-Summary-02-June-21.pdf

United Nations (2017) Transforming our world: the 2030 Agenda for Sustainable Development. Accessed 14 November 2021, from https://sustainabledevelopment.un.org/content/documents/21252030%20Agenda%20for%20Sustainable%20Development%20web.pdf

University of Edinburgh (2021) Common racial microaggressions. Accessed 14 November 2021, from www.ed.ac.uk/equality-diversity/students/microaggressions/racial-microaggressions/common-racial-micro-agressions

Varnum, M. E. & Grossmann, I. (2017) Cultural change: The how and the why. *Perspectives on Psychological Science*, 12(6), 956–72.

Verma, A. (2020) Intersectionality, positioning and narrative: exploring the utility of audio diaries in healthcare students' workplace learning. *International Social Science Journal*, 70(237–8), 205–19.

Virdee, S. & McGeever, B. (2018) Racism, crisis, Brexit. *Ethnic and Racial Studies*, 41(10), 1802–19.

Williams, M. T. (2020) Psychology cannot afford to ignore the many harms caused by microaggressions. *Perspectives on Psychological Science*, 15(1), 38–43. DOI: 10.1177/1745691619893362.

Williams, M. T. (2021) Racial microaggressions: critical questions, state of the science, and new directions. *Perspectives on Psychological Science*, 16(5), 880–5.

Wodak, R. & Reisigl, M. (2015) Discourse and racism. In D. Tannen, H. E. Hamilton & D. Schiffrin (eds), *The Handbook of Discourse Analysis* (pp 576–596). Malden, MA: John Wiley & Sons.

PART II

Staff experiences of racism

2

Academic staff experiences

Min Duchenski, Tamjid Mujtaba and Jalpa Ruparelia

Introduction

Academic staff are critical to the HE system, contributing both original knowledge and scholarship to schools of thought and subjects of study. The role of academic staff has changed considerably with them now engaged in governance, lead roles, publishing, delivering research and teaching excellence, conferences and curriculum development, among a few areas (Graham, 2015). This chapter explores the different aspects of academic staff experience.

Despite various policy changes and anti-racism frameworks in many HEIs, systemic institutional racism continues to make Black, Asian, and minority ethnic[1] academics feel like they are excluded and discriminated against (ECU, 2011; Pilkington, 2013; Alexander & Arday, 2015; UCU, 2016). While navigating the inequitable landscape of academia, Black academics face a 'culture of explicit and passive bullying [that] persists across higher education along with racial stereotyping and racial microaggressions' (Rollock, 2019, p 4).

While some progress has been made in HEIs with regards to addressing race equality, Pilkington (2013) argues that the rhetoric surrounding policy making and recruitment should not seduce us into believing that HEIs are sufficiently addressing racism. Little difference is being made for Black, Asian and minority ethnic academics, as many HEIs fail to turn well-written policy into meaningful action. The Equality Challenge Unit (ECU, 2011) highlighted the disparities between the experiences of Black and minority ethnic staff in higher education (HE) and the policies and strategies designed to promote race equality. Recently, the McGregor-Smith Review (2017) identified discrimination and bias against individuals from Black, Asian and minority ethnic backgrounds at every stage of their careers. A year on from the review, Kerr's (2018) Scorecard Report highlighted that ambitious Black, Asian and minority ethnic individuals in the workplace were facing lack of opportunity, thus wasting their talent, enthusiasm and expertise in the sector. The University and College Union (UCU, 2016) found that most Black, Asian and minority ethnic academics surveyed had reported facing barriers to promotion. These barriers included not being fully informed on the application process for promotion, as well as a lack of support from senior colleagues and managers in seeking career progression. Unsurprisingly, Black, Asian and minority ethnic academics were and still are more likely than White colleagues to consider leaving their current HEI to work elsewhere and/ or abroad in order to progress their careers (Bhopal, Brown & Jackson, 2016).

Where experiences of racism in the recent past were often overt and violent, it is also more subtle, deeply embedded into institutions and at times referred to as 'unconscious'. In research examining the lived experiences of Black, Asian and minority ethnic academics working in UK universities, Bhopal (2015) reported experiences that were covert, subtle forms of discriminatory practice, rather than overt racial discrimination and exclusion. Respondents highlighted differences in standards applied to their performance compared with White colleagues, namely, lack of trust, over-scrutinisation and questioning of credibility (Bhopal, 2015). Additionally, a vast majority (over 70 per cent) of Black, Asian and minority ethnic academics surveyed by UCU (2016) reported bullying or harassment from managers and colleagues, exclusion from decision making and experiences of cultural insensitivity.

Academics from Black, Asian and minority ethnic backgrounds are under-represented in senior, decision-making roles, and the lack of career progression of Black, Asian and minority ethnic academics remains an urgent concern (Arday, 2021). According to 2018/19 data, the Higher Education Statistics Agency (HESA, 2020) reported that out of a total of more than 21,000 professors, only 140 were Black (less than 1 per cent), 1,360 were Asian (6 per cent), 2,000 were unidentified or from another ethnic background, while the majority (nearly 18,000) were White (85 per cent). These statistics were almost identical to the HESA data in 2012/13 (HESA, 2014), indicating that little has changed in the past five years. In 2016, UCU reported that only three of 159 heads of HEIs were from Black, Asian and minority ethnic backgrounds. The intersectional experiences of many academics also contribute to this inequality, with most UK HEIs not employing any professors that are women from Black, Asian and minority ethnic backgrounds, and in 2017 there were just 54 Black, Asian and minority ethnic women professors in the whole of the UK (Runnymede Trust, 2017).

The evidence showcases that a career in academia continues to be dominated by a White patriarchy and in order to succeed in this world, Black, Asian and minority ethnic academics must navigate their way through microaggressions and/or macroaggressions in order to find liberation and success. We note that microaggressions by academic staff take many forms. For example, covert racial aggressions can take the form of setting up meetings on widely known religious festivals, asking Black, Asian and minority ethnic colleagues 'where do you come from?', suggesting that they do not belong to this country, or within academia making statements such as 'you have done well given where you have come from'. This statement indicates that Black, Asian and minority ethnic people are not usually expected to be found in academia, historically reserved for White people. More overt racial aggressions are experienced when Black, Asian and minority ethnic staff are asked about their religious attire. For example, female Muslim staff are asked 'why do you wear the hijab?' or 'doesn't it feel hot in there?' or 'how can you fast – doesn't it impact your thinking?', which enables other people to perpetuate a 'you do not belong, and you are not one of us' culture. Other microaggressions are even more covert in nature. This is highlighted in examples of Black, Asian and minority ethnic staff being referred to as 'assistants' or 'mentees' by senior academics when all the while little or no mentoring is provided; instead Black, Asian and minority ethnic staff are being used to enhance the careers of senior White HE leaders in undertaking performative tasks. Another example is the way in which Black, Asian and minority ethnic staff are often told to 'stay in their lane' in the HE hierarchy and this can result in blocking access to building up cases for promotion and career success. This can often take the form of no exposure to networking, or no invitation to contribute to external seminars/talks, books or chapters, or to collaborate on grant proposals.

Voice of a peer

In the years I have been working in HE, I have felt a complete lack of belonging in academia. When I joined HE, I was unaware at the time that I was experiencing 'imposter syndrome'. I did not feel qualified enough for the role I had acquired (despite ticking the boxes on paper). In order to 'not be found out' I would stay quiet in meetings, feeling that I had lost my voice (despite my previous 14 years in education), I would respond to work requests without a fuss and in general, behave like the good little Indian girl I had been raised to be. I frequently felt very conscious of being the only person of colour in the room and experienced examples of subtle discrimination on numerous occasions. Nevertheless, I threw myself into the job and felt I was working twice as hard as most White colleagues, to 'prove' my worth.

I slowly found my feet and completed my first year as an academic but went on maternity leave the following year. When I returned a year later, I had lost even more confidence, returning to a stressful environment that was not just unwelcoming to a person of colour, but hostile to women with young families. The intersectional experience as an Asian female left me feeling more isolated than I had before and I felt like I was being punished for having a child. I had been breastfeeding while on maternity leave and prior to returning to work I asked my head of department if I could have a room in which I could express breast milk to continue breastfeeding. I was told that there was a public 'family room' I could use, or I could use the 'disabled toilets'. I felt completely unsupported and was horrified that to get privacy I would need to use an unhygienic space. I expressed (excuse the pun!) my concerns but was ignored and I ultimately felt I had little choice, so made the difficult decision to stop breastfeeding.

In the summer of 2018, I was sent an email with the subject heading 'strong Black and minority ethnic student from this year's cohort' from a more senior colleague asking if I could suggest the names of some students who 'fit the categories', as per the request from an even more senior colleague. The email request from this senior academic had been forwarded, asking for a 'recent articulate graduate' to speak at an event, followed by 'currently the panel is looking a little White'. Angered by the tokenistic effort at equal opportunities I replied, expressing my concerns that selecting students on the grounds of race was unconducive to equal opportunities, especially if the students were aware that they had been selected due to their race. I highlighted that this was a particularly sensitive issue at that time, as some Black, Asian and minority ethnic students on the course had reported experiences of racism (from staff and other students) throughout that academic year. I did not receive a reply from my colleague and an Asian student was selected to speak on the panel.

On reflection, I can understand the desire for a representative panel indicated that efforts were being made to be more inclusive. However, the whole incident, including the fact that I had been selected (as the only woman of colour in the whole academic programme) to find the 'Black and minority ethnic student', alongside the lack of response to my concerns, left me feeling angry and upset, and that yet again my voice was not being heard.

In a separate incident, I was conversing with members of my department regarding an issue I was having with HR. A more senior White colleague walking by the office at the time popped in to say hello, having listened in on some of the conversation. The senior academic suggested that I "send an email to HR", because as soon as they saw my surname they would respond straight away. The suggestion being made here was that my non-English surname would somehow lead to positive discrimination. The looks that the other members of my department gave each other and to me confirmed this suspicion. This brief, yet significant, incident left me feeling ashamed, not just because I could somehow benefit from my surname, but that I did not challenge the comments that were made due to fear and embarrassment. Regardless of the 'advice' given from my senior colleague, I have found quite the opposite in practice. My emails are being systematically ignored by HR and by my Union over a pay dispute that has been going on for the last five months. I can't help but wonder if this dispute would have been resolved by now (or at least my emails would have been responded to) if I had a more English-sounding surname.

The series of events discussed previously have left me feeling bitter, mostly because I did little to challenge them. Through attending webinars on anti-racism and reading literature on the 'ivory tower', I have reflected on my personal identity and simultaneously realised that I am not alone in my experiences. Through uniting with other Black, Asian and minority ethnic academics and White allies, I feel empowered to use my voice in promoting anti-racism and channel my bitterness and anger into positive change.

Change domains

Supporting and championing Black, Asian and minority ethnic academics in recruitment and career progression

HEIs should take action that supports the recruitment and progression of individuals from Black, Asian and minority ethnic backgrounds. Black, Asian and minority ethnic staff need to feel empowered to resist marginalisation and therefore make meaningful career progression (Gabriel, 2013; Gabriel & Tate, 2017). Action should include a raised awareness of how career opportunities can be accessed by those from Black, Asian and minority ethnic backgrounds, purposeful mentoring and coaching programmes to support Black, Asian and minority ethnic staff development being offered, as well as encouragement and assistance to Black, Asian and minority ethnic staff in applying for promotions through appropriate professional guidance. HEIs should monitor the number of Black, Asian and minority ethnic staff that apply for roles, as well as those that undergo successful promotion. If there is an underrepresentation of Black, Asian and minority ethnic individuals that are recruited and promoted, then the HEI should take appropriate measures to investigate and address this.

Training in equality, diversity, inclusion and meaningful implicit bias

Positive change in understanding and practicing anti-racism requires hard work, effort and commitment on everyone's part and so HEIs need to demonstrate long-term strategies to address race equality for progress to be made. It may be the case that those academic staff that most need training will not attend workshops on EDI; therefore, training should be compulsory for all staff regardless of their grade and seniority. Workshops on 'White fragility' that highlight implicit bias and address microaggressions faced by Black, Asian and minority ethnic staff (for instance, understanding why questions such as 'Where are you originally from?' are derogatory) would help academics working towards race equality. The Equality Challenge Unit (ECU) (2013) have produced training packs on unconscious bias that could be utilised to inform actions to address these behaviours. All academics should be encouraged to reflect on their hidden biases, such as through Implicit Association Tests (IATs) developed by psychologists as part of 'Project Implicit' (Greenwald, Banaji & Nosek, 2015).

Recognising and acknowledging academic White privilege and power

There should not be a fear of facing further discrimination or criticism for whistle-blowing in instances of harassment and bullying. White allies should be encouraged to challenge racist comments (whether they are direct or indirect) in their support of anti-racism. All staff (and students) in HEIs should be able to work in an inclusive, equitable, equal and diverse workplace that is free from bullying and harassment. Therefore, appropriate policies must be implemented and adhered to, to ensure all Black, Asian and minority ethnic academic staff are able to reach their full potential.

Strategies that promote 'colour blindness' have not been successful in advancing race equality (Apfelbaum et al, 2010;

Eberhardt, 2019). It is important for senior leaders in HEIs to recognise and collectively challenge the discrimination that Black, Asian and minority ethnic staff face. Black, Asian and minority ethnic staff should be seen and consulted on issues regarding race equality, with the principles of 'no decision about us without us', in a similar approach to the government's vision of putting patients first and empowering health professionals in their White Paper 'Equity and Excellence: Liberating the NHS', with shared decision making and 'no decision about me without me' being the norm (Department of Health, 2010, p 1). It is important, therefore, that there is visible representation of Black, Asian and minority ethnic staff on decision-making panels. Consequently, Black, Asian and minority ethnic staff should not be treated as a homogenous community, but rather recognised and celebrated not only for multicultural differences, but also other factors that contribute to their intersectional experiences, such as gender, age, social class, sexual orientation and religion.

Dismantling a racist system requires White colleagues and counterparts to take positive action to fight racism. Celebrating the differences within all members of staff comes in part from allyship. Recognition of White privilege and how this could be used to benefit Black, Asian and minority ethnic staff is important, by being a voice of support and educating others within academia. This can take the pressure away from Black, Asian and minority ethnic staff that are consistently and exhaustingly relied upon to provide answers and definitions of racial terminology, as well as the racial aggressions that they face.

Creating safe spaces and learning communities for academic staff

Black, Asian and minority ethnic staff should be given opportunities to discuss their negative experiences of racism and marginalisation, whether this is through town hall meetings or through anonymous reporting (Black, Asian and minority ethnic staff should be consulted on what medium they would prefer). Such experiences could inform where staff development is needed in HEIs and therefore could be used as a tool to regularly update race equality frameworks and policy documents.

By creating safe spaces, HEIs may be supporting those from Black, Asian and minority ethnic backgrounds in creating a partnership and a sense of personal and professional belonging. Furthermore, learning communities, which actively encourage dialogue, could support Black, Asian and minority ethnic staff in their professional development.

When institutions seek to formulate actions against racist behaviours and attitudes towards Black, Asian and minority ethnic academics, much of it is hidden behind equality and diversity policies. Although relevant and valid, it must be queried whether such policies have a meaningful impact. Ahmed (2012, p 114) writes of the need for 'commitment', which is 'a state of being bound to a course of action or to another person or persons'. Black, Asian and minority ethnic colleagues need to be able to express their feelings of being seen as the 'other', with White colleagues who actively listen and reflect on their own behaviours. The commitment must extend beyond policies to actions to ensure in every meeting at any level there is discussion on issues to do with race to enable deeper learning and communication. This does not mean that racism will disappear; time and energy is necessary for translating commitment to action, but every individual must face up to the fact that most institutions are places of White privilege where Black, Asian and minority ethnic staff are marginalised. However, a challenge is that doing this will mean that speaking about racism will lead to White people being 'hurt by what is heard as a charge, such that the charge becomes about their hurt' (Ahmed, 2012, p 147).

Examining and reforming racist employment practices, promotions and professional development

Pilkington (2013) states that recruitment policies and practices appear to be transparent with clear criteria for shortlisting and appointments, and continues by stating that 'formal procedures can act as a smokescreen for judgements which may be indirectly discriminatory' (p 230) because of the selection process. Most academic appointments expect a presentation as part of the interview process, and this is when 'indirect discrimination' can play a part. Candidates are judged on their abilities to fit into a team or a department, and Black, Asian and minority ethnic candidates seem to fall short in this regard (Pilkington, 2013; Sian, 2017). Joseph-Salisbury (2019) takes this argument further and affirms that not employing Black academics 'acts to reinforce the notion that intellectualism is the preserve of Whiteness' (p 8), but if there are these invisible barriers of not being seen to 'fit in', how can we tackle this? Recruitment practices, interview panels and selection processes must be challenged systemically, and training should be provided on anti-racist recruitment and selection practices.

Issues about recruitment and selection seem to impact Black, Asian and minority ethnic women in particular (Sian, 2017; Joseph-Salisbury, 2019; Bhopal & Pitkin, 2020). Bhopal and Henderson (2019) analysed HEIs' involvement in race and gender initiatives and found that gender took precedence over race. Therefore, when institutions feel compelled to discuss race, they revert to 'easier' topics such as gender and this is reflected in the data and representation of women professors. Nearly 24 per cent of professors are White and female, whereas only 2.1 per cent are Black, Asian and minority ethnic female professors in the UK (Bhopal, 2020). Much of this is due to a lack of relevant mentoring for female Black, Asian and minority ethnic academics (Sian, 2017), as well as a lack of opportunity or support for career progression (Shilliam, 2015; UCU, 2016). There needs to be a drive to understand and integrate intersectionality (Crenshaw, 1989) within all university committees and at senior executive level in a bid to understand the complexities of race and anti-racist policies and practices. The Race Equality Charter (REC) may help to push forward institutional changes but only if management is proactive in adopting an anti-racist stance with the appropriate financial support, in a similar way to how Athena Swan has led to changes for women in HEIs (as highlighted by Bhopal & Henderson, 2019).

With regards to drafting and implementing policies and procedures, Black, Asian and minority ethnic staff should be represented or included either physically or through consideration of issues to do with equality, diversity, inclusion and race. These aforementioned terms need to be analysed in depth, but as far as including alternative perspectives when writing policies, there can be no argument against this move. Ahmed's (2012) research into who takes on 'diversity work' highlights the problems associated with such work: academics may ignore recommendations from diversity committees and practitioners or see the policies as irrelevant to their work as they believe they are not racist. Another issue Ahmed (2015) uncovered is the institutional bias in translating policy to practice because the policy documents may have been evaluated as being of an excellent standard; therefore the institution was also considered to be excellent in managing diversity. Pilkington's (2011) case study on institutional racism at a British university led to a critical conclusion that policies are drawn up and implemented from a White perspective, and therefore change is difficult to implement.

Reflective questions

- How have you applied learning from EDI training to support Black, Asian and minority ethnic academic staff?
- Are you aware of racist incidents (overt and covert/indirect) that Black, Asian and minority ethnic academic staff have experienced in your HEI? If so, what was done to address these?
- How often are equality policies monitored and evaluated in relation to Black, Asian and minority ethnic academic staff?
- How do senior leadership teams reconcile themselves to the fact that Black, Asian and minority ethnic academics feel like outsiders and unsupported in their career choices?
- Are you aware of White privilege in your academic role?
- Are you an ally for Black, Asian and minority ethnic academics?
- Are you aware of the microaggressions and macroaggressions that Black, Asian and minority ethnic academics face daily?
- How could you support Black, Asian and minority ethnic academic colleagues in being anti-racist?
- Are you aware of what it means to share your power and privilege with Black, Asian and minority ethnic academics?
- Are all student views given equal opportunity to be aired when they witness unfair treatment of Black, Asian and minority ethnic academics, and are these views are escalated to be actioned? How do students communicate their concerns and to whom?

Note

[1] It is recognised that the reference to the expanded BAME label for academics is contentious, as Black, Asian and minority ethnic individuals do not belong to a homogenous group, each having vastly different experiences within academia (in addition to intersectional experiences). Black, Asian and minority ethnic is used for the purpose of this review in referring to non-White individuals or people 'of colour', with regards to their marginalisation and racism experienced within academia.

References

Ahmed, S. (2012) *On Being Included: Racism and Diversity in Institutional Life*. Durham, NC: Duke University Press.

Ahmed, S. (2015) Doing diversity work in higher education. In C. Alexander & J. Arday (eds), *Aiming Higher: Race, Iinequality and Ddiversity in the Aacademy*. London: Runnymede Trust. Online Accessed 22 July 2020, from https://www.runnymedetrust.org/uploads/Aiming%20Higher.pdf

Alexander, C. & Arday, J. (eds) (2015) *Aiming Higher: Race, Inequality and Diversity in the Academy*. London: Runnymede Trust. Accessed 22 July 2020, from www.runnymedetrust.org/uploads/Aiming%20Higher.pdf

Apfelbaum, E. P., Pauker, K., Sommers, S. R. and Ambady, N. (2010) In Blind Pursuit of Racial Equality? *Psychological Science*, 21(11), 1587–92.

Arday, J. (2021) Fighting the tide: Understanding the difficulties facing Black, Asian and minority ethnic (BAME) Doctoral Students' pursuing a career in Academia. *Educational Philosophy and Theory*, 53(10), 972–979. DOI: 10.1080/00131857.2020.1777640.

Bhopal, K. (2015) The experiences of black and minority ethnic academics: multiple identities and career progression. In C. Alexander & J. Arday (eds) (2015). *Aiming Higher: Race, Inequality and Diversity in the Academy*. London: Runnymede Trust. Accessed 23 July 2020, from www.runnymedetrust.org/uploads/Aiming%20Higher.pdf

Bhopal, K. (2020) UK's white female academics are being privileged above women – and men – of colour. Accessed 19 February 2022, from https://research.birmingham.ac.uk/en/publications/uks-white-female-academics-are-being-privileged-above-women-and-m

Bhopal, K. & Henderson, H. (2019) Advancing equality in higher education: an exploratory study of the Athena SWAN and Race Equality Charters. *British Academy/Leverhulme Research Report*. Birmingham: University of Birmingham.

Bhopal, K. & Pitkin, C. (2020) 'Same old story, just a different policy': race and policy making in higher education in the UK. *Race Ethnicity and Education*, 23, 530–547. DOI: 10.1080/13613324.2020.1718082.

Bhopal, K., Brown, H. & Jackson, J. (2016) BME academic flight from UK to overseas higher education: aspects of marginalisation and exclusion. *British Educational Research Journal*, 42(2), 240–57.

Department of Health (2010) *Equity and Excellence: Liberating the NHS. White Paper*. London: Department of Health and Social Care. Accessed 30 July 2020, from www.gov.uk/government/publications/liberating-the-nhs-White-paper

Eberhardt, J. L. (2019) Science: The 'colorblind' approach to racism doesn't work: you cannot make your kids non-racist by pretending race doesn't exist. In Eberhardt, J. L. (ed) (2019) *Biased: Uncovering the Hidden Prejudice That Shapes What We See, Think and Do*. New York: Viking. Accessed 30 July 2020, from https://lithub.com/science-the-colorblind-approach-to-racism-doesnt-work/

ECU (Equality Challenge Unit) (2011) *The Experience of Black and Minority Ethnic Staff in Higher Education in England*. London: Equality Challenge Unit.

ECU (Equality Challenge Unit) (2013) *Unconscious Bias and Higher Education*. London: Equality Challenge Unit.

Equality and Human Rights Commission (2019) *Experiences. Tackling Racial Harassment: Universities Challenged*. Equality and Human Rights Commission. Accessed 19 Febuary 2022, from www.equalityhumanrights.com/sites/default/files/tackling-racial-harassment-universities-challenged.pdf

Gabriel, D. (2013) Self-empowerment is the best way to defeat racism in academia. *The Independent*. Accessed 23 July 2020, from www.independent.co.uk/student/news/self-empowerment-is-the-best-way-to-defeat-racism-in-academia-8582702.html

Gabriel, D. and Tate, S. A. (2017) Inside the Ivory Tower: Narratives of Women of Colour Surviving and Thriving in British Academia. London: UCL IOE Press.

Graham, A. T. (2015) Academic staff performance and workload in higher education in the UK: the conceptual dichotomy. *Journal of Further and Higher Education*, 39(5), 665–79.

Greenwald, A. G., Banaji, M. R. & Nosek, B. A. (2015) Statistically small effects of the Implicit Association Test can have societally large effects. *Journal of Personality and Social Psychology*, 108(4), 553–61. DOI: 10.1037/pspa0000016.

HESA (2014) *Higher Education Staff Statistics: UK, 2012/13*. London: HESA.

HESA (2020) *Higher Education Staff Statistics: UK, 2018/19*. London: HESA.

Joseph-Salisbury, R. (2019) Institutionalised whiteness, racial microaggressions and black bodies out of place. *Higher Education, Whiteness and Education*, 4(1), 1–17. DOI: 10.1080/23793406.2019.1620629.

Kerr, S. (2018) The Scorecard Report: Race at Work 2018: The McGregor-Smith Review One Year On. London: Business in the Community. Accessed 23 July 2020, from https://assets.publishing.service.gov.uk/government/uploads/system/uploads/attachment_data/file/746970/BITC_Race_At_Work_Report.pdf

McGregor-Smith (2017) Race in the Workplace: The McGregor-Smith Review. London: Government Department for Business, Energy & Industrial Strategy. Accessed 22 July 2020, from www.gov.uk/government/publications/race-in-the-workplace-the-mcgregor-smith-review

Pilkington, A. (2013) The interacting dynamics of institutional racism in higher education. *Race Ethnicity and Education*, 16(2), 225–45.

Rollock, N. (2019) *Staying Power: The Career Experiences and Strategies of UK Black Female Professors*. London: University and College Union. Accessed 23 July 2020, from www.ucu.org.uk/media/10075/Staying-Power/pdf/UCU_Rollock_February_2019.pdf

Runnymede Trust (2017) Black Female Professors in the UK. London: Runnymede Trust. Accessed 23 July 2020, from https://www.runnymedetrust.org/blog/black-female-professors-in-the-uk

Shilliam, R. (2015) Black academia: the doors have been open but the architecture remains the same. In C. Alexander & J. Arday (eds), *Aiming Higher: Race, Equality and Diversity in the Academy*. London: The Runnymede Trust. Accessed 23 July 2020, from www.runnymedetrust.org/uploads/Aiming%20Higher.pdf

Sian, K. P. (2017) Being black in a white world: understanding racism in British universities. *Papeles del Centro de Estudios sobre la Identidad Colectiva*, 1–26. Accessed 23 July 2020, from http://eprints.whiterose.ac.uk/121107/8/SIAN_corregido_autora_1.pdf

UCU (University and College Union) (2016) *The Experiences of Black and Ethnic Minority Staff in Further and Higher Education*. London: University and College Union. Accessed 23 July 2020, from www.ucu.org.uk/media/7861/The-experiences-of-black-and-minority-ethnic-staff-in-further-and-higher-education-Feb-16/pdf/ucu_bmesurvey_report_feb16.pdf

3

Professional and support services staff

Claire Lee

Introduction

This chapter focuses on professional and support services staff and the issues of racism faced by them in their day-to-day work. Professional and support services staff play a crucial role in the day-to-day running of university business and systems. With the modernisation of HEIs, an agile workforce is considered crucial to the growth of HEIs and resilience.

At a university, strategic areas such as student recruitment employ large numbers of professional and support services staff, and this is noted as a major trend across the HE sector (Baltaru, 2019). Baltaru argues that this increase is a reaction to the increasing nature of internationalisation and marketing agendas for HEIs (for example Baltaru & Soysal, 2017). In order to meet the increasing operational needs associated with a larger student body, universities rely heavily on staff on fixed-term contracts (Baltaru, 2019). According to Batty (2020), more than 50 per cent of staff are typically in insecure employment. Currently, as a 'substantial cost-saving initiative', some universities are reported as not renewing contracts of fixed-term employees (Courtois, Lauder & Watermeyer, 2020). According to HESA[1] (2021) 2019/20 data, there are no Black, 20 Asian, 5 mixed and 25 unknown employees classified in managerial, director and senior official posts, in contrast to 435 White staff. Of the

221,545 staff noted in professional occupations, 165,755 are White, 4,700 are Black, 21,930 are Asian, 5,010 are mixed and 19,225 are not known. The HESA data does not provide a full picture, indicating that only 131 of 197 HE providers opted into returning data about non-academic staff. Despite a large number noted in professional occupations, the lack of representation in non-academic services in manager, director and senior official posts is a concern.

Discussions and studies have circulated around employment in HE. Brown and Sessions (2006) have concluded that the type of employment contract has a strong influence on the attitudes and satisfaction of employees towards their jobs. More specifically, fixed-term employees are relatively less secure and optimistic about their professional future (Brown & Sessions, 2006). The racialised experiences and adversities of professional and support staff are uniquely different to those in academic posts, and the pressures of working in environments focused on transformation and change management can often prohibit professional and support staff from opportunities and progression (an issue noted in Brown & Sessions, 2006).

Voice of the author

I was first recruited into HE as part of a National Collaborative Outreach Programme (NCOP) to deliver outreach activity to Widening Participation (WP) students. Feeling disenchanted with outreach work, I applied for a role with the EDI team. Although the contract was for five months, I believed that the role had the power to levy change at the university and that the contract would be extended.

Upon starting at EDI, I realised that I was one of three people of colour in a 60-person office. I rarely saw my line manager or team, which consisted of three other members. Whereas I imagined taking concrete actions to combat racial injustice at the university, in reality I was pushing paper for my line manager. Trapped in a stifling bureaucratic prison, we were expected to meet targets under approaching deadlines, most of which were past the end of my contract. Questions about contract extensions or the future of EDI work were dismissed. Any ideas I wanted to progress always failed because senior executives did not give us the buy-in we needed to promote the importance of race equality.

The tension between the EDI team and the rest of the office was an elephant in the room. I felt colleagues visibly reduce me to my ethnicity and gender: "Of course you're in the EDI team: you're Black, Asian and minority ethnic", a colleague remarked. When sending out meeting invitations to the Race Equality monthly meetings, I received rejections regularly. "Is this a required meeting?" was a question I was asked often.

It was clear that my efforts were not making a dent in race equality work, and that my contract would not be extended. I spent much of my time trying to hastily finish reports while being preoccupied with securing another job. I realised how much the institution failed me, and that race equality work would never succeed without the buy-in of senior champions.

Change domains

The race/Black, Asian and minority ethnic network of a university having a senior champion or sponsor

Each network of a university should have a senior champion to have buy-in and immediate endorsement. In this way, the network can leverage support for Black, Asian and minority ethnic fixed-term employees who seek out the network for solidarity and support. Such sponsorship from a senior leader can help ensure that staff are seen, heard and meaningfully represented in senior meetings. This is particularly important for professional and support services staff to ensure they feel they are able to participate in decisions that impact their experience, retention, recruitment and success working in HE.

All human resources, professional and support staff members requiring attendance at race equality training

As professional and support staff numbers continue to grow in HEIs, disparities may continue to widen and diverse representation continue to fall, particularly as we see an unclear pathway for Black, Asian and minority ethnic professional and support services staff to progress in HEIs. While training is not the only solution to addressing racial disparities across professional and support services staff functions, embedding such training into institutional systems can ensure that there is a good standard of knowledge in translating race equality theory into action. The intention of this is to help change the culture of the university to take racial justice more seriously.

Assigning a non-academic mentor and a human resources representative/partner to fixed-term employees

Employees on fixed-term contracts can often be brought in for specific projects and tasks, where their wellbeing and professional development can often be neglected. Providing fixed-term staff with a buddy, mentor and/or professional partner can help ensure such staff have support and guidance from the institution and increase their sense of belonging despite their intended length of service. Fixed-term employees can also be empowered to have the option to air their grievances, seek support and receive help in finding another position.

Reflective questions

- What race equality networks/areas of the university have you championed and formally sponsored to empower professional and support services permanent and contract staff?
- How have you started to consider positive action in your recruitment and retention plans for professional and support services staff in your organisation?
- How many race equality and intersectionality trainings have you attended and what have you carried through your committed actions to understand the experiences of Black, Asian and minority ethnic professional and support services staff?
- What wellbeing measures do you have in place for staff, and students, racialised as Black, Asian and minority ethnic on fixed-term contracts?
- How have you contributed to the ongoing development of race equality and diversity content that your professional and support services staff are exposed to at the university?

Note

[1]   www.hesa.ac.uk/data-and-analysis/staff/working-in-he/characteristics

References

Baltaru, R. (2019) Universities' pursuit of inclusion and its effects on professional staff: the case of the United Kingdom, *Studies in Higher Education*, 77, 641–56. DOI: 10.1007/s10734-018-0293-7.

Baltaru, R. & Soysal, Y. (2017) Administrators in higher education: organizational expansion in a transforming institution, *Studies in Higher Education*, 76, 213–29. DOI: 10.1007/s10734-017-0204-3.

Batty, D. (2020) Hundreds of university staff to be made redundant due to coronavirus. *The Guardian*, 2 April. Accessed 22 July 2020, from www.theguardian.com/education/2020/apr/02/hundreds-of-university-staff-made-redundant-due-to-coronavirus?utm_term=Autofeed&CMP=twt_gu&utm_medium&utm_source=Twitter#Echobox=1585815904

Brown, S. & Sessions, J. (2006) Employee attitudes, earnings and fixed-term contracts. *International Evidence, Review of World Economics*, 141(2), 296–317.

Courtois, A., Lauder, H. & Watermeyer, R. (2020) Reacting to Covid-19 by slashing fixed-term staff would be a disaster. *Times Higher Education*, 3 April. Accessed 22 July 2020, from www.timeshighereducation.com/opinion/reacting-covid-19-slashing-fixed-term-staff-would-be-adisaster#

HESA (2021) Table 3 – HE staff by activity standard occupational classification 2014/15 to 2019/20. Accessed 28 July 2021, from www.hesa.ac.uk/data-and-analysis/staff/table-3

PART III

Student experiences of racism

4

Undergraduate student experiences

Josephine Gabi and Sonia Gomes

Introduction

This chapter focuses on all undergraduate students and the issues of racism faced by this student group in their university journey. In the chapter, we highlight Black and ethnic minority undergraduate students' experiences of racism and racialisation in UK HEIs. The chapter is based on the premise that daily aggressions, racial and discriminatory challenges that are encountered by Black and minority ethnic students are often unacknowledged and not effectively addressed (for example, Haynes-Baratz et al, 2021 and Bunce et al, 2019). This has led to a student campaign for universities to decolonise the curriculum, calling out practices and processes that perpetuate cognitive imperialism – 'Why is my curriculum White?' (NUS, 2016) – and improved racial representation – 'Why isn't my professor Black?' (Black, 2014). Most universities' response to these demands has been pledging action with no tangible, visible commitment to eradicating racism properly (Denovan & Macaskill, 2013; Reay, 2018). This highlights the failure of institutions to meet the learning needs of these students as they cater to the privileged White students (Le Roux & Moller, 2002). These consciously and unconsciously textured practices and processes perpetuate the status quo. This is further reproduced by a Eurocentric curriculum that silences and erases

Black and minority ethnic students' cultural capital, histories and experiences as it perpetuates the reproduction of subjectivities of Whiteness (Arday, 2018).

Despite an increase in the number of students entering HE with similar requisite qualifications, and socioeconomic and educational backgrounds, Black students report lower levels of satisfaction compared with other racial groups and are also more likely to 'drop out' and have lower attainment and/or awarding levels than their White peers (Joseph-Salisbury, 2018). The dominant view on the degree-awarding gap is dismissive of race and racism as a contributory factor to this persistent inequity (Madriaga, 2017). The impact of racism on Black and minority ethnic students is pervasive and has far-reaching physiological and psychological consequences such as race-based stress, trauma and 'racial battle fatigue' (Franklin, 2019).

According to NUS (2010), even when Black and ethnic minority students enter HE on a level playing field with similar entry requirements, they are likely to achieve worse degrees than their White peers. This has a knock-on effect on their graduate employment gap, which is worse compared with their White counterparts (HEFCE, 2018). This gap in turn leads to an ethnicity pay gap and intergenerational economic disadvantage. Ash et al (2020) observe that 'racism continues to persist in higher education and traditional diversity initiatives that focus only on support resources and tolerance training continue to fall short in making lasting change' (p 1). This matter of racial justice and equity calls for HE institutions to be responsive to this systematic epistemic violation.

Voice of the author

My participation in this chapter is rooted in my ethical responsibility, commitment to social justice and equity experience. Since I started teaching in HE, I have consistently been involved in interfaculty student support, which has contributed towards equity and student outcomes. Most of this work has been mentoring students from diverse backgrounds who often encounter challenges when exploring issues around race, ethnicity and racialisation. I find myself in an entanglement of both my present experience as an academic staff member and my previous one as an undergraduate student. Throughout my three years as an undergraduate student on the course, most of what I learnt was from a Eurocentric perspective. In instances where tutors provided examples of children from Africa, these were often images on PowerPoint presentations of impoverished children with flies in their eyes or an almost naked child holding a machete. Although tutors facilitated analytical discussions around these depictions, explaining that such images were not representative of all children in Africa, it still left an indelible mark on my students' perceptions. At the end of the session, my peers would often ask me to explain how my own childhood was affected by poverty growing up in Africa. The lack of a diverse range of voices in the HE curriculum, particularly in knowledge produced in the Global South, has meant that students were not always provided with sufficient tools to engage meaningfully with these complex and multi-layered narratives. Where assessment tasks involved analysing case studies, these were mostly set in the cultural and socio-historical context of White British children and family. This did not afford possibilities for me to explore my childhood experience or that of children and families from a Zimbabwean context. Such epistemological orientation imposed racially biased ways of being and knowing that privileged my White British peers whose subjectivities were prioritised, albeit subconsciously. Peters (2015) notes that such 'lack of awareness that the curriculum is White composed of "White ideas" by "White authors" is a result of colonialism that has normalised Whiteness and made Blackness invisible' (p 641). This systemic academic invisibility and unequal recognition evoke otherness. The need for curriculum transformation, learning and teaching that is locally grounding and globally relevant is not only urgent, but it is a social justice and equity issue.

Change domains

Developing racial literacy

Issues related to race and racialisation are constructed using language in HE. Therefore, a consideration of terminology that is used to describe students is important as it also influences decisions on initiatives that are aimed at meeting their needs.

The following shows an outline of key racial terminology in HE institutions that should be asserted when designing actions to tackle racism with students:

- Learn and acknowledge the occurrence of institutional racism when policies and practices of an organisation unfairly discriminate against students from Black, Asian or other minority ethnic backgrounds or groups (Nadgee, 2019; Olanisakin, 2020). This can occur without conscious intention and even well-intentioned acts could be considered racist if they have racist consequences (Soyei, 2019, p 2).
- Challenge the 'BAME' label, which is typically and conveniently used to describe people of non-White descent, which is problematic as in the context of HE, this implies that these students are a homogenous group. The category 'Black, Asian and minority ethnic' 'also overlooks the fact that African, Asian and all non-White people are a global majority' (National Education Union, 2020).
- Tackle the 'Black, Asian and minority ethnic attainment gap', which is a racial inequality in UK universities and the NUS (2019); therefore, efforts that are aimed at addressing this differential outcome should not emanate from a deficit view that blames students but rather tackle structural inequalities that underlie this. When race ('Black, Asian and minority ethnic') is viewed as the source of the student 'attainment gap', and is framed from a deficit perspective, it relinquishes institutions from responsibility (Berry & Locke, 2011). Thus, it is imperative to engage in ceaseless probing conversations about the use of terminology and how it impacts on perceptions about students and their needs.
- Sponsoring curriculum transformation is important, and a Eurocentric curriculum marginalises Black and minority ethnic students as it assumes perceived docility, making them feel they are in university to be enlightened instead of legitimately contributing to the co-production of knowledge where all students equally participate in knowledge exchange and sharing insights. Culturally sustaining pedagogy and curriculum transformation that decentre Western perspectives engages all students in a meaningful and socially just way.

Dismantling the glass ceiling of achievement

HEIs do not produce equal outcomes for all students. The degree-awarding gap (known as the Black, Asian and minority ethnic attainment gap) is seen from a deficit perspective that suggests Black and minority ethnic students need fixing through remediation. They are often unfairly judged as not possessing intellectual skills and attributes to attain good degree classifications. This view detracts from the centrality of endemic racism, racialisation and Islamophobia in HE as it 'absolves the institution of any responsibility or requirement to reflect on or change its practices' (Wilson & Jones, 2020). By not acknowledging structural inequalities that underpin the differential outcomes, institutions perpetuate racial violence and aggressions through a range of institutional and individual practices. Such use of ethnicity/race (and labels such as 'BAME' that describe students of non-White descent) as indicators of perceived academic deficiency propagates stereotypical prejudice, institutional microaggressions, race discrimination and otherness, and is not only dehumanising but is an epistemic injustice that nurtures inferiority and delegitimises the knowledge, experiences and histories of students based on race. There is no evidence to suggest that intellectual abilities are connected to the amount of melanin racially minoritised students have. Therefore, the degree-awarding gap is a glass ceiling for academic achievement that 'needs to be acknowledged as a racial inequality' (UUK and NUS, 2019, p 38). Universities should be held accountable for underserving Black and ethnic minority student communities through practices and processes that contribute to the differential outcomes. This is, therefore, an urgent matter of social justice and equity and institutions have 'a legal responsibility to ensure equal opportunities for those with any of the nine protected characteristics of the Equality Act 2010' (UUK and NUS, 2019, p 38). To address this inequity:

- Acknowledge the existence of an unlevel playing field and systemic inequality that undergirds the degree-awarding gap and address 'race and racialised factors affecting students, albeit with acknowledgment of other intersections where these might be contributory factors' (UUK and NUS, 2019, p 38). This is a necessary shift towards avoiding intergenerational reproduction of systemic inequity.

- HE is based on Eurocentric epistemic canon that legitimises Western-centric ways of knowing and being that subjugate knowledge, histories and experiences of Black and ethnic minority students and treat them as passive recipients of knowledge within the White-led and designed curriculum, which makes it epistemically disempowering.

- Acknowledge students' prior knowledge, experiences and histories by developing a curriculum that appreciates multi-layered intersectional issues, for example, race, gender, disability, sexuality and class.

- Some HE institutions currently use anonymous marking. This is an acknowledgement of conscious and unconscious bias in assessment processes. It does not address the devaluation of students' academic work on race and ethnicity even when anonymously assessed. It, therefore, detracts from the centrality of racism/racial prejudice that should be dismantled by bringing to consciousness subtle forms of bias. Existing unconscious bias training does not account for systemic and structural issues that enable assessment biases to be perpetuated with no accountability for perceived unconscious decisions.

Race-based stress and trauma

Black and minority ethnic students disproportionately experience race-based stress and trauma and 'racial battle fatigue' (Franklin, 2019) due to ceaseless experiences of inequity they encounter. As observed by Mirza (2018, p 183) these are some of the costs of 'just being there', which their White peers may never experience. Institutions should therefore:

- Train staff on 'how to manage situations in which there is an imbalance of power rooted in racial or religious oppression' where 'hostile exchanges, leave Black and minority ethnic students feeling undermined, unvalued, isolated and subsequently withdrawn' (Akel, 2019, p 32) helps minimise the re-traumatising of students, disparities in academic outcomes and dropout rates.

- Provide a curriculum that encourages discussions about race and racism and why it matters (Anderson et al, 2019).
- Improve racial representation by recruiting Black and minority ethnic staff and ensure the provision of affective and culturally sustaining teaching that benefits all students.

Sense of belonging

While there has been a concerted effort to widen participation and entry into HE of students from underrepresented groups, there has been negligible university commitment to tackle racial and intersectional discrimination that is encountered by Black and ethnic minority students. Black and minority ethnic students' attrition rates compared with their White peers are persistently higher (Lawton, 2018). Contributory factors include a lack of cultural connection to the curriculum, difficulties making friends with students from other ethnicities and difficulties forming relationships with academic staff due to the differences in background and customs (Bulman, 2017). Identification of these multiple interacting factors that impact on student experience and ability to 'stay on' to degree completion would potentially help develop students' sense of academic and social belonging and curb the attrition rates. Institutions tend to be socially and culturally biased, privileging dominant cultures, which in turn, even if subconsciously, influences interactions between staff and students and among students and assessment processes. Developing a sense of belonging can be addressed through:

- 'Integrating, social and academic elements of university life encourage students to build relations with each other and with staff and to engage with the curriculum' (Goldsmiths Students Union, 2019). This may help build a community of learners and a sense of connection to the university.
- HE learning and teaching is multifaceted and affective. With such a diverse student population entering with unique characteristics, circumstances, experiences and knowledge, the interaction between the institutional environment and their

personal experiences, histories and knowledge consequently shapes understandings of reality and educational experience. Therefore, recognition of personal tutoring as part of personal, professional and academic endeavour, and not remedial, will go some way towards student retention, progression and success. The effectiveness of this approach will require cultural transformation (Singh, 2011).

- The affective dimension of learning and teaching with the embedding of personal tutoring and academic advising would help welcome students into HE in a hospitable and humanistic way, where they feel valued as humans first before they are learners. Such an approach would place equal importance on student academic and human needs. The underpinning assumption here is that learner needs are unlikely to be catered for where human needs are not overlooked in the intricately interwoven web of human needs.

- Another function of personal tutoring and academic advising would be putting in place risk identification protocols for early identification of, and early intervention in, potential student alienation and attrition vulnerability.

Reflective questions

- What language do you use to describe Black, Asian and ethnic minority students?[1]
- How will you ensure that language, practices and processes accurately and responsibly capture, acknowledge and tackle systemic racism and microaggressions?[2]
- What strategies are you using to close the degree-awarding gap (the Black, Asian and minority ethnic attainment gap) in your institution?[3]
- Why are there so few Black and ethnic minority role models in university structures in your institution yet so many students from Black and minority ethnic backgrounds (Olonisakin, 2020)?[4]
- As a manager, director and/or senior official, it is your job to eradicate racism:
    - Why is the data from anti-racism research not made use of and their recommendation not yet implemented?

* Why are you not training your own staff to contribute to and cultivate an increasing diversity pool?
- In what ways does teaching and research appreciate the lived experiences and realities of Black and ethnic minority students and not only take racism as a term and concept to be analysed and deconstructed but rather taught and researched with intent to dismantle racism?[5]
- How do you decolonise, deracialise and degender the curriculum, learning, teaching and research in order to generate possibilities of opening spaces for the blossoming of liberated scholarly thought (Black, 2019)?[6]
- What tools do you have in place to evaluate whether teaching or research is part of the solution or problem?[7]
- What is knowledge and what do you accept as knowledge? Who is in control of knowledge? How do you facilitate the co-production of knowledge?
- How will you ensure that the classroom is a compassionate space for all students?[8]
- What stops you from initiating and taking part in discussions about equitable and inclusive pedagogy to bring about change?
- What is keeping you from embracing anti-racism pedagogy?
- Why are you not proactively developing and providing training that promotes collaborative learning between staff and students?
- What will it take for you to speak out in the face of an injustice and oppressive systems?[9]
- Are you aware of your institution's procedure to report racism?[10]
- Racism is bigger than the individual: are you connecting with others often enough to get and provide support and find ways to combat racism?
- What keeps you from challenging the coloniality of knowledge?

Notes
[1] Acronyms such as BAME can dehumanise Black and minority ethnic students who are targeted by racism. The acronym 'BAME' is a governmental category of reports. Used in an HE institution, it homogenised the experiences and histories of students targeted by racism.

Most students do not identify with the label Black, Asian and minority ethnic. Such ethnic glossing is unethical as it disfigures and conceals students' individuality.

2   Terms such as 'inclusion' and 'diversity' are often used by different institutions. These terms should be put under erasure. There is an assumption that the term 'inclusion' equates with equity, but 'inclusion' often centres the privileged White as the norm and the ones with entitlement to extend the invitation and inclusion of Black and minority ethnic who are viewed as other and docile recipients of the favour. 'Diversity' as a term can be a euphemism that obscures the role that White supremacy plays in diversity, perceptions of difference and anti-Blackness.

3   Racial and social equity is everyone's ethical responsibility. Often Black and ethnic minority staff and students are involved in talks about dismantling racism without institutional acknowledgement of the emotional labour and psychological trauma this exposes them to, particularly if they do not have the tools to dismantle racism. As observed by Audre Lorde (1984) 'the master's tools will never dismantle the master's house'.

4   Racial representation and diversity of voices expand and enrich student experience. Intellectual inferiority of Black and minority ethnic people is ceaselessly being perpetuated by the lack of representation in HE, where Whiteness is seen as the standard (Madriaga, 2017).

5   Freire (1968, p 19) observes that 'all education is political; teaching is never a neutral act', hence the need for teaching and research staff to be conscious of their own positionality, orientation and knowledge that have the pretension of universality and neutrality (Bartolome, 2008).

6   Designing units, compiling reading lists and planning sessions entail narrating stories. How these stories are told, which actors are privileged and placed at the centre and whose voices are authoritative and viewed as part of the academic canon while others are silenced and marginalised are all important considerations in learning, teaching and research.

7   Teaching (and research) has the potential to contribute to the development of anti-racist, decolonial and hospitable process-oriented learning that allows multiple realities, histories, knowledge, skills, ways of being and doing to co-exist, critically interact and reinforce each other while genuinely and profoundly acknowledging, respecting and appreciating difference.

8   Conversations about race and racism often involve unequal degrees of risk for different students. For Black and minority ethnic students this may be emotionally exhausting and for White students threatening. Conversations about race are important as they enable students to appreciate the reasons why certain experiences and histories are privileged to the detriment of others. Therefore, for spaces to be safe, they must be free from violence as a precondition for students' emotional, psychological and discursive safety.

9   Black and minority ethnic students may not challenge instances of discrimination because of fear of being victimised. To be able to speak out, it is important to be sufficiently equipped to recognise daily macroaggressions and systemic racism and an awareness of the unequal consequences of

speaking up on racism for different students. Solidarity is important in achieving racial equity.

[10] Policy and procedure for reporting racism should be available to all students and explained clearly. Imagine if we did not know the number '999' to call in the event of a medical emergency – what would happen? Racism is a physical and mental health emergency; it is therefore imperative to report it (Bhui et al, 2018).

References

Akel, S. (2019) *Insider-Outsider: The Role of Race in Shaping the Experiences of Black and Minority Ethnic Students.* London: Goldsmith University of London.

Anderson, R. E., Saleem, F. T. & Huguley, J. P. (2019) Choosing to see the racial stress that afflicts our Black students. *Phi Delta Kappan*, 101(3), 20–25. Accessed 20 June 2020, from https://kappanonline.org/racial-stress-black-students-anderson-saleem-huguley/

Arday, J. (2018) Dismantling power and privilege through reflexivity: negotiating normative Whiteness, the Eurocentric curriculum and racial micro-aggressions within the Academy. *Whiteness and Education*, 3(2), 141–61.

Ash, A. N., Hill, R., Ridson, S. N. & Jun, A. (2020) Anti-racism in higher education: a model for change. *Race and Pedagogy Journal*, 4(3), 1–35.

Bartolome, L. I. (ed) (2008) *Ideologies in Education: Unmasking the Trap of Teacher Neutrality.* New York: Peter Lang.

Berry, J. & Loke, G. (2011) *Improving the Degree Attainment of Black and Minority Ethnic Students.* London: The Equality Challenge Unit/Higher Education Academy.

Bhui, K., Nazroo, J., Francis, J., Halvorsrud, K. & Rhodes, J. (2018) *The Impact of Racism on Mental Health.* London: Synergi Collaborative Centre.

Black, D. (2019) Decolonising the medieval curriculum: critical questions. Accessed 22 July 2019, from https://daisyblack.uk/decolonising-the-medieval-curriculum-critical-questions/

Black, L. N. (2014) *Why Isn't My Professor Black? On Reflection.* Race Matters: Runnymede. Accessed 20 June 2020, from www.runnymedetrust.org/blog/why-isnt-my-professor-black

Boutta, M. (2015) Beyond the gap: dismantling institutional racism, decolonising Education. In C. Alexander and J. Arday (eds) *Aiming Higher: Race, Inequality and Diversity in the Academy.* London: Runnymede Trust.

Bulman, M. (2017) Black students 50% more likely to drop out of university, new figures reveal. *The Independent.* Accessed 20 June 2020, from www.independent.co.uk/news/uk/home-news/black-students-drop-outuniversityfigures-a7847731.html

Bunce, L., King, N., Saran, S. & Talib, N. (2019) Experiences of black and minority ethnic (BME) students in higher education: applying self-determination theory to understand the BME attainment gap. *Studies in Higher Education,* 46(3), 534–547.

Denovan, A. & Macaskill, A. (2013) An interpretative phenomenological analysis of stress and coping in first year undergraduates. *British Educational Research Journal,* 39(6), 1002–24.

Equality and Human Rights Commission (2019) *Experiences. Tackling Racial Harassment: Universities Challenged.* Accessed 20 June 2020, from www.equalityhumanrights.com/sites/default/files/tackling-racial-harassment-universities-challenged.pdf

Franklin, J. D. (2019) Coping with racial battle fatigue: differences and similarities for African American and Mexican American college students. *Race Ethnicity and Education,* 22(5): 589–609. DOI: 10.1080/13613324.2019.1579178.

Goldsmith Students Union (2019) Retention – why students drop out and what we can do about it. Devised, researched, and written by students. Accessed 22 July 2020, from www.goldsmithssu.org/asset/News/6013/RETENTION.pdf

Haynes-Baratz, M. C., Metinyurt, T., Li, Y. L., Gonzales, J. & Bond, M. A. (2021) Bystander training for faculty: a promising approach to tackling microaggressions in the academy. *New Ideas in Psychology,* 63, 100882.

Higher Education Funding Council for England (2018) Differences in student outcomes: the effect of student characteristics. Accessed 23 July 2020, from www.hefce.ac.uk/pubs/year/2018/201805/

Joseph-Salisbury, R. (2018) Whiteness characterises higher education institutions – so why are we surprised by racism? Accessed 20 July 2020, from https://theconversation.com/Whiteness-characterises-higher-education-institutions-so-why-are-we-surprised-by-racism-93147

Lawton, G. (2018) Why do black students quit university more often than their White peers? *The Guardian.* Accessed 20 July 2020, from www.theguardian.com/inequality/2018/jan/17/why-do-black-students-quit-university-more-often-than-White-peers

Le Roux, J. & Moller, T. (2002) No problem! Avoidance of cultural diversity in teacher training. *South African Journal of Education,* 22(3), 184–7.

Madriaga, M. (2017) Whiteness, academic achievement, and misrecognition in English HE. At 11th Critical Race Studies in Education Association Annual Conference, Indianapolis, Indiana, USA, 31 May–2 June 2017 (unpublished).

Miller, M. (2016) *The Ethnicity Attainment Gap: Literature Review.* Sheffield: University of Sheffield: Widening Participation Research and Evaluation Unit.

Mirza, H. S. (2018) Black bodies 'out of place' in academic spaces: gender, race, faith and culture in post-race times. In J. Arday & H. S. Mirza (eds) *Dismantling Race in Higher Education: Racism, Whiteness and Decolonising the Academy.* London: Palgrave.

Moran, S. (2004) White lives in focus: connecting social praxis, subjectivity and privilege. *Borderlands,* 3(2), 1–10.

Nagdee, I. (2019) Universities must stop covering up racism in order to protect their own reputations. *The Guardian.* Accessed 20 July 2020, from www.theguardian.com/education/2019/oct/23/universities-must-stop-covering-up-racism-in-order-to-protect-their-own-reputations

National Education Union (2020) Framework for developing an Anti-racist approach. Accessed 20 July 2020, from https://neu.org.uk/media/11236/view

National Union of Students (2010) Race for Equality: A report on the experiences of black students in further and higher education. Accessed 23 July 2020, from www.nus.org.uk/PageFiles/12350/NUS_Race_for_Equality_web.pdf

National Union of Students (2016) Why is my curriculum White? Decolonising the academy. Accessed 22 July 2020, from www.nusconnect.org.uk/articles/why-is-my-curriculum-White-decolonising-the-academy

Olonisakin, F. (2020) Universities can and should do much more to address systemic racism. *Times Higher Education.* Accessed 20 July 2020, from www.timeshighereducation.com/opinion/universities-can-and-should-do-much-more-address-systemic-racism

Peters, M. A. (2015) Why is my curriculum White? *Educational Philosophy and Theory*, 47(7), 641–6.

Reay, D. (2018) Race and elite universities in the UK. In *Dismantling Race in Higher Education* (pp 47–66). Cham: Palgrave Macmillan.

Singh, G. (2011) *Black and Minority Ethnic (BME) Students' Participation in Higher Education: Improving Retention and Success.* London: Higher Education Academy.

Soyei, S. (2019) *The Barriers to Challenging Racism and Promoting Race Equality in England's Schools.* Tyne & Wear: Show Racism the Red Card.

Universities UK and National Union of Students (2019) Black, Asian and minority ethnic student attainment at UK Universities: #closingthegap. Accessed 20 July 2020, from www.universitiesuk.ac.uk/policy-and-analysis/reports/Documents/2019/Black,Asian and minority ethnic-student-attainment-uk-universities-closing-the-gap.pdf

Wilson, M. A. & Jones, L. (2020) Dear senior university leaders: what will you say you did to address racism in higher education? *Times Higher Education.* Accessed 20 June 2020, from www.timeshighereducation.com/blog/dear-senior-university-leaders-what-will-you-say-you-did-address-racism-higher-education

5

Postgraduate student experiences

Arun Verma

Introduction

This chapter focuses on all postgraduate students and the issues of racism faced by these students in their university journey. Postgraduate (PG) students who are engaged in taught and research programmes experience their education uniquely compared with the undergraduate student. Broadhead et al (2020) explored Black, Asian and minority ethnic students' experiences of postgraduate degrees, highlighting critical concern about the widening gap in degree continuation rates 'where only 83% of BAME students continued their studies compared with 90% of White students' (p 2). Furthermore, Black, Asian and minority ethnic postgraduate students were found to feel less engaged with the curriculum due to its Eurocentricity, isolated and lacking in confidence to discuss race issues with White staff (Broadhead et al, 2020).

Although racism is pervasive in the postgraduate student experience, it is noted that postgraduate students will typically have more opportunities, be exposed to more placements and opportunities to practise skills and may often have closer contact with academic and professional leads than at undergraduate level (Donaldson & McNicholas, 2004). However, racism in the postgraduate experience is often surrounded by White supremacy in the university environment and space (Ahmet,

2020), with international students experiencing direct racist abuse leading to 'sadness, disappointment, homesickness and anger' (Brown & Jones, 2011, p 1). I also highlight the role of doctoral students who identify as Black, Asian and minority ethnic and experience racism that can often adversely impact their retention and success during their doctorates (for example, Avery-Desmarais et al, 2021). For example, data shows that '245 (1.2%) [doctorates] were awarded to Black or Black Mixed students, with just 30 of those being from Black Caribbean backgrounds' (Leading Routes, 2019, p 3). It is highlighted in evidence that a lack of diverse and authentic representation is a barrier to engaging Black, Asian and minority ethnic doctoral candidates, where 'the racial microaggressions is carefully articulated through subtle persistent daily reoccurrences which attempt to position faculty of colour as incapable or inferior to their White counterparts' (Arday, 2021, p 975).

Voices from literature

> This is the (name of university) that everybody knows. That everybody imagines before they step foot on the campus. This is the University of the rich. The University of the well-to-do. The University of future heads of state, future Nobel laureates and world changers. This is the University of faux radicalism, where the Marxists ask what you have read rather than what you think. People in high places ask what makes us a part of the university? That which makes you part of the university is that which makes you apart from most of the world. Most people on earth aren't White and neither am I, most people on earth can't afford the fees and neither can I. (Extract from Ahmet, 2020)

> On my first day of classes, I asked a question to a lecturer about how a theory on identity that she spoke about during the lecture relates to race and gender. She quickly got defensive and after another student of colour spoke up on my behalf, she stated

that she was not going to 'get into an argument'. Before coming to university, I made the decision that I would not become the 'angry black woman' in my classes. I thought the lecturer and I were having a discussion about theory, but she must not have seen it that way and on my first day of classes at university, in front of the entire department, I was seen as 'getting into an argument'. I became the argumentative, angry black woman on the first day of classes. I doubt the lecturer even remembers this interaction, but I haven't forgotten it. (Extract from Ahmet, 2020)

Change domains

Reforming White spaces and environments for postgraduates

Universities need to reconsider and reassess the physical embodiment of White supremacy[1]and White privilege[2] in postgraduate spaces to enhance access and inclusivity for prospective and current postgraduate students. Such spaces can exclude Black, Asian and minority ethnic students from belonging and feeling included in what can be high-pressured environments in the postgraduate student setting. Introducing and embedding diverse representation in physical and virtual spaces and cultivating further inclusive cultures on campuses and beyond are required.

Research supervisors, principal investigators and external examiners need to engage in regular anti-racist coaching and/or training

The purpose of this change is to ensure that core academic staff who supervise students closely are recognising and addressing racism in their approach, with a focus on improving, informing and shaping graduate outcomes. Ensuring that White academics are not collecting or tokenising the global majority would help postgraduate research candidates to enhance their social optics or brand to receive more funding and status in their careers. The impact of supervisory relationships breaking down has been documented for decades (for example, Hockey, 1996). However, recent debate has shed light on the adverse impact of dysconscious racism,[3] which can contribute to postgraduate student attrition and racial trauma (Walker, 2020).

Reassessing and reforming monitoring committee panels in universities

Redesigning the monitoring committee process can help ensure that Black, Asian and minority ethnic identifying postgraduate students are safe to share and whistle-blow racist experiences without fear of penalty. Postgraduate students who do speak the truth to power can often be reprimanded by senior academics through creating cultures of fear. Particularly for Black candidates, this can lead to the 'misalignment [becoming] filled with inequity, tension and oppression, culminating in the relationship breakdown' and enable doctoral students to drop out (Walker 2020).

Reflective questions

- How are you ensuring that your PG students racialised as Black, Asian and minority ethnic can have the same access, opportunity and fairness that White students have as they study?
- How will you transform your doctoral supervision mechanisms for support to be tailored to those who identify as Black, Asian and minority ethnic?
- What meaningful and authentic welcome packs and experiences are made to prospective and new students of colour in your PG students?
- How can you ensure that PG students' admission processes enable them to feel part of the university and treated with dignity and respect?
- Can we ensure that the placements we approve for PG students that engage in work-based learning are appropriate to the student and support them as a person of colour?
- How as a student and group are you including Black and minority ethnic peers during your postgraduate journey?

Notes

[1] 'White supremacy describes a historically contingent system of power in which White people disproportionately have access to power and privilege at the expense of racially minoritised people' (Mills, 1997, as cited in Joseph-Salisbury, 2019).

[2] 'White privilege is the benefits that you get from being White. If you are an ethnic minority there are certain disadvantages you have. ... It doesn't mean you haven't earned your successes, but it does mean that your life hasn't been harder because of the colour of your skin' (BBC, 2020).

[3] 'Dysconscious racism is an uncritical habit of mind that lacks any ethical judgment regarding or critique of systemic racial inequity. By unquestioningly accepting the status quo, this mind-set, which is identified as an outcome of miseducation, prevents teachers, for example, from questioning the existing racial order and leaves no room for them to imagine practical possibilities for social change or their role as change agents' (Banks, 2012).

References

Ahmet, A. (2020). Who is worthy of a place on these walls? Postgraduate students, UK universities, and institutional racism. *Area*, 52, 678–686. DOI: 10.1111/area.12627.

Arday, J. (2021). Fighting the tide: understanding the difficulties facing Black, Asian and minority ethnic doctoral students pursuing a career in academia. *Educational Philosophy and Theory*, 1(8), 972–979. DOI: 10.1080/00131857.2020.1777640.

Avery-Desmarais, S. L., Revell, S. M. H. & McCurry, M. K. (2021) A theoretical framework to promote minority PhD and DNP student success in nursing education. *Journal of Professional Nursing*. 37(6), 1149–53.

Banks, J. A. (2012) Dysconscious racism and teacher education. In *Encyclopedia of Diversity in Education* (Vol. 1, pp 724–6). London: SAGE Publications, Inc. Accessed 1 December 2021, from www.doi.org/10.4135/9781452218533.n225

BBC (2020) White privilege: what is it and how can it be used to help others? Accessed 28 July 2021, from www.bbc.co.uk/newsround/52937905

Broadhead, S., Bale, I., Case, K., Hussain, M. & Woolley, D. (2020) Exploring the black, Asian and ethnic minority (BAME) student experience using a Community of Inquiry approach. *Journal of Widening Participation and Lifelong Learning*, 22(1), 112–31.

Brown, L. & Jones, I. (2011) Encounters with racism and the international student experience. *Studies in Higher Education*, 38(7), 1004–19.

Donaldson, B. & McNicholas, C. (2004) Understanding the postgraduate education market for UK-based students: a review and empirical study. *International Journal of Non-Profit and Voluntary Sector Marketing*, 9(4), 346–60.

Hockey, J. (1996) A contractual solution to problems in the supervision of PhD degrees in the UK. *Studies in Higher Education*, 21(3), 359–71.

Joseph-Salisbury, R. (2019) Institutionalised whiteness, racial microaggressions and black bodies out of place in Higher Education. *Whiteness and Education*, 4(1), 1–17.

Leading Routes (2019) *The Broken Pipeline: Barriers to Black PhD Students Accessing Research Council Funding*. London: UCL/ Leading Routes.

Mills, C. W. (1997) *The Racial Contract*. London: Cornell University Press.

Walker, S. (2020) Racism in academia: (how to) stay black, sane and proud as the doctoral supervisory relationship implodes. In *The International Handbook of Black Community Mental Health*. Bingley: Emerald Publishing Limited.

6

Student social experiences

Zoe Nutakor

Introduction

This chapter focuses on the issues of racism during social gatherings faced by all student groups during their university journey, and refers to involvement in clubs/societies, graduate balls and university events.

The social experience within British universities is in many ways a product of the inherent White middle-class nature of these institutions (Arday & Mirza, 2018). Universities were born out of elitism, only those with significant wealth and/or socioeconomic status being able to access a higher level of education (for example, Maesse, 2017). It can be said that being ingrained in British culture is at the detriment of all others (that is, Lentin, 2018). University societies are widely considered to be a staple of the university social experience, so we must consider the Black, Asian and minority ethnic experiences of these groups (Ahn & Davis, 2020). Societies foster practices such as 'Black face' and racist drinking games, as they take an 'anything goes' approach to humour (as highlighted by Reclaim the Campus, 2020). These are considered by White students to be an unfortunate by-product of an otherwise fun gathering; the mental strain and frustration faced by Black, Asian and minority ethnic students as a result cannot go ignored. Indeed, to ignore these frustrations is to ignore the intersecting identities and feelings of Black, Asian and minority ethnic students, which can be considered racist within itself (for example, Reclaim the Campus, 2020). Racism is not confined to public-facing ventures with university social bubbles; there have been many reports of racism within individual interactions (for example, Ahmet, 2020). It is not uncommon for terms such as 'chink', 'Paki' and/or 'n★★★★r' to be hurled at Black, Asian and minority ethnic students, which is often dismissed as humour, or an alcohol-fuelled mistake (for example, Kmietowicz, 2020). White students regularly fail to use their Black, Asian and minority ethnic peers' proper names, or express difficulty pronouncing them as though it is the fault of the name holder (for example, Gamsu, Donnelly & Harris, 2019). A common question to be asked is "where are you from?", which is racially insensitive and undermines the supposed multicultural nature of university spaces and cultures. The issue of racial gaslighting can also undermine students' experiences of addressing and tackling racism on campus (for example, Applebaum, 2020; Johnson et al, 2021). It is these aggressions that adversely shape the social experiences of students on campus, and even through virtual learning, and these are further brought to life in the following sections.

Voice of the author

As a mixed White and Black African undergraduate student at Durham University, I am surrounded by White faces in college and in societies. I discovered on fresher's week that my race made me stick out like a sore thumb. On my third night in Durham, I was approached by a White, male fellow fresher, who proceeded to grab my hair and tell me it was awesome. He saw this as the way to initiate a sexual encounter, channelled by a racialised fetish – my African hair. To be confined to a xenophobic idea of an exotic being in such a scenario is detrimental to one's self-esteem. I was told "don't let anyone make you feel bad about your hair" by a mixed-race male while volunteering outside two of Durham's nightclubs, as a mutual understanding. My college, St Cuthbert's Society, is Durham's third oldest. While it does attempt to be progressive, many of its historical traditions are rooted in a notion of British excellence. I consider the expectation to join in with the college song to be a form of Whitewashing – my culture became lost in the chant. While in a nightclub, I was made to feel 'uncool' for liking rap music, as my excitement at the sound of Stormzy's 'Vossi Bop' was greeted with a murmur of "I don't like it". My culture was quashed. I have struggled with certain societies, as they present key social justice issues considering their White experience. For example, my college's feminist society mentioned the importance of race within their discussion, but then proceeded to focus on their own personal experiences, with my own being ignored.

Racist socials and events

The following image (Figure 6.1) has been identified from the public domain as perpetuating racist social experiences for students and illustrates a visual example of racism. This was an image identified from UAL Truth[1] who gave permission to use it for the book:

Figure 6.1: Instagram post illustrating racism in university social invitations

Change domains

Zero-tolerance policy

The idea of a zero-tolerance policy may sound daunting, but it does not require a mass exclusion of students accused of racist behaviours. This should operate at a university, student union, and society level (also at college level if your institution is collegiate). Potential sanctions can include but are not limited to a temporary or permanent ban from the relevant area of the university social sphere, a letter of apology to the victim(s), a letter of reflection, a strike policy, restricting participating in university activities and a reflective session considering their behaviour. To be as effective as possible, I recommend that anti-racism policies operate as a network across all spheres of the student union and wider university, to tackle the issue effectively and prevent any racist behaviours seeping through the cracks. This would mean that a college, or its equivalent, would tackle racism in exactly the same manner as a society. Lack of efficiency and inconsistency too often allows racist incidents to fall under the radar, which only aggravates the issue. A shift such as this will lead to fundamental change.

Anti-racism workshops

These should be made compulsory to all students arriving at and/ or returning to university, with the view to inciting an anti-racist mindset from the outset. I would recommend splitting students into two groups, with White students attending an anti-racism and White privilege workshop, and Black, Asian and minority ethnic students attending a workshop which also focuses on self-perception and self-care in response to racism. Reflection forms or feedback from small group leaders would be useful at the end of each workshop to ensure progress has been made. These workshops should be authored and delivered by Black, Asian and minority ethnic staff and student leaders, with resources written by Black, Asian and minority ethnic individuals. The charity Show Racism the Red Card[2] is a useful resource, as well as the books cited in the references of this chapter. If the content of the workshop is of good quality, it will shake White students from their previous mindset, as it is likely they have not previously had their perceptions of race challenged in this way.

Positive action

I will not hesitate to say that students of all ethnic backgrounds are equally capable and valuable as student leaders, and that includes White students. However, there is the inescapable issue of bias against Black, Asian and minority ethnic students. It is not uncommon for ethnic minority students to be dismissed, undermined, criticised and outvoted when they put themselves forward to lead their peers within societies and the wider student union. Positive action could involve outreach such as social media campaigns and drop-ins held by societies to support and encourage Black, Asian and minority ethnic students' runs for elections (for example., Vizi, 2017). These voices at the forefront will almost certainly filter into the rest of the society and lead to a more positive and welcoming atmosphere for other Black, Asian and minority ethnic students.

Celebrations of Black, Asian and minority ethnic culture

This recommendation is given for the primary benefit of Black, Asian and minority ethnic students, as they otherwise have their culture overlooked as a result of the inherently British nature of HEIs. An example is a formal event or ball that serves food and plays music from a specific Black, Asian and minority ethnic group. This should not be an extra event, but instead should serve as part of the fabric of the university social scene. For example, if there is an annual charity ball, this ball can be adapted to also be a cultural celebration. This will sit well with the students from Black, Asian and minority ethnic backgrounds, as it will create a sense of familiarity, as opposed to the sometimes inhospitality of more traditional events. These will also certainly help with cultural appreciation, as White students will experience the best of other cultures, and the enjoyment of the event will be synonymous with this. Charity events should involve acknowledgement of the countries affected as valued homes worthy of cultural celebration, rather than wastelands that need renovation.

Reflective questions

- To what extent is the traditional, historic element of your institution born out of ideas of empire and supremacy? Is this to the detriment of the minority cultures it was built on?

- Are the Black, Asian and minority ethnic students at your institution merely a statistic? What have your interactions with these students been thus far and what could you learn from them?
- What might have led you to perhaps treat the social experiences of ethnic minority students as secondary until now?
- What might prevent a Black, Asian and minority ethnic student from reporting a racist incident within their university social life?
- What is the quality of the current support they could expect to receive?
- How ready would you be to challenge racist comments you overheard directed at a Black, Asian and minority ethnic student?
- When giving talks in an extracurricular setting, do you consider the implications of the topic or the event itself on the Black, Asian and minority ethnic students participating?
- Are your lectures and tutorials a safe place for Black, Asian and minority ethnic students, which facilitate a safe social atmosphere for them?
- Does your work have a direct or indirect impact on the social life of the students at your institution? If so, how often have you considered race issues when planning and making decisions?
- Do you see race issues as a part of student welfare?
- Do you play music tailored to different ethnic groups? Will all students be able to feel included with the entertainment and events you put on?
- How do you respond to Black, Asian and minority ethnic students talking about race issues? Why might it cause you discomfort?
- How do you respond to Black, Asian and minority ethnic fashion and hairstyles? Is it always culturally sensitive?

Notes

[1] UAL Truth is a social media profile self-described as an anonymous safe space for BIPOC UAL students/ex-students/staff to voice their experiences (https://www.instagram.com/ualtruth/)
[2] https://www.theredcard.org/

References

Ahmet, A. (2020) Who is worthy of a place on these walls? Postgraduate students, UK universities, and institutional racism. *Area*, 52, 678–686. DOI: 10.1111/area.12627.

Ahn, M. Y. & Davis, H. H. (2020) Four domains of students' sense of belonging to university. *Studies in Higher Education*, 45(3), 622–34.

Applebaum, B. (2020) The call for intellectual diversity on campuses and the problem of willful ignorance. *Educational Theory*, 70(4), 445–61.

Arday, J. & Mirza, H. S. (eds) (2018) *Dismantling Race in Higher Education: Racism, Whiteness and Decolonising the Academy*. Cham: Springer.

Gamsu, S., Donnelly, M. & Harris, R. (2019) The spatial dynamics of race in the transition to university: diverse cities and white campuses in UK higher education. *Population, Space and Place*, 25(5), e2222.

Johnson, V. E., Nadal, K. L., Sissoko, D. G. & King, R. (2021) 'It's not in your head': gaslighting, splaining, victim blaming, and other harmful reactions to microaggressions. *Perspectives on Psychological Science*, 16(5), 1024–36.

Kmietowicz, Z. (2020) Are medical schools turning a blind eye to racism? *BMJ*, 368, m420. DOI: 10.1136/bmj.m420.

Lentin, A. (2018) Beyond denial: 'not racism' as racist violence. *Continuum*, 32(4), 400–14.

Maesse, J. (2017) The elitism dispositif: hierarchization, discourses of excellence and organizational change in European economics. *Higher Education*, 73(6), 909–27.

Reclaim the Campus (2020) Racism at UK universities. Accessed 28 July 2021, from www.reclaimthecampus.com/post/racism-at-uk-universities

Vizi, B. (2017) Positive action, the prohibition of discrimination, and minority rights from a European perspective. *Compilation of Lectures: Ensuring Equality and Preventing Discrimination on Ethnic Grounds* (pp 68–83). Flensburg: European Centre for Minority Issues.

PART IV

Research systems enabling racism

7

Research funding and contracts

Arun Verma

Introduction

This chapter interrogates the pervasion of racism in research funding, with regards to issues faced by staff in bidding for and managing research grants and contracts with local, national and international partnerships (Li et al, 2021). There are racial disparities of research grants and bids reflected in the number of grants awarded to Black, Asian and Ethnic minority researchers in HE being much lower than to White applicants for research funding. Contracts and funding in research collaborations are considered here as areas for change, particularly with regards to managing funding and contracts with integrity and eliminating racism through vetting, while ensuring research contracts are held with partners that champion anti-racism or are on an explicit journey to becoming anti-racist. We know that

> in the UK, senior researchers from an ethnic minority are half as likely to have success with a research funding application as their White peers, according to figures from UK Research and Innovation (UKRI) for the financial year 2018–2019. And if they succeed, they get £564,000 on average, versus £670,000 for White researchers. (Murugesu & Vaughan, 2020)

The recent UKRI calls for research on Black, Asian and minority ethnic communities affected by COVID-19 have also not awarded any projects led by Black academic applicants (Inge, 2020). The funders play a critical role in perpetuating racism and colonialism with 'some funders [finding] the language of structural racism too controversial or political and are unlikely to support work that puts the issue front and centre' (Brown et al, 2019, p 5).

In a recent report it was found that:

> in all categories of applications, between 8–10% of applicants do not disclose their ethnicity. White applicants form most applicants, although there is an increase in ethnic minority applicants for CIs and Fellows since 2014/15:
>
> - In 2018/19 UKRI received 1,215 applications from PIs from ethnic minorities (13%) and 7,460 applications from White applicants (79%). This pattern has remained relatively steady since 2014/15 when the proportion of ethnic minority applicants was 11% and that of White applicants was 81%.
> - In 2018/19, UKRI received 550 applications for response mode funding from those in ethnic minorities and 3,655 from White applicants. In 2018/19, most of the ethnic minority (55%) applicants applied to managed mode calls.
> - In 2018/19, UKRI received 5,950 (22%) application from CIs from ethnic minorities and 17,985 (68%) applications from White applicants. This is an increase of 10 percentage points for ethnic minority CIs from 12% in 2014/15.
> - In 2018/19, UKRI received 280 (16%) Fellowship applications from ethnic minorities, compared to 1,310 (75%) from White applicants. The 4pp increase in the share of ethnic minority applications masks annual fluctuations. (My Science Inquiry, 2019)

The data reflects significant disparities of those that receive and are successful in securing research funding and grants, which not only facilitates staff and institutions' contributions to society but can have a critical impact on how staff are retained and are enabled to progress in their careers. Additionally, recent evidence submitted to the Diversity in STEM inquiry has highlighted the disparities of ethnic minority underrepresentation and disparities in research funding decision making (Ramnani, 2022).

Voices from literature

A lecturer in cardiovascular sciences at the University of Leeds, UK, says she isn't surprised by the findings [that ethnic minority academics get less funding], and that they reflect her experiences as a tenured academic. Before she was awarded a UKRI leadership fellowship this year, she had nine consecutive fellowship applications and grant proposals rejected. (Murugesu, 2019)

We are concerned and disillusioned to learn that a major British funding organisation which made an explicit commitment to equality, and which is legally bound by the public sector equality duty act (PSED), awarded £0 of £4.3 million to Black academic leads (in a UKRI and NIHR funded study) to explore COVID-19 and its disproportionate impact on Black, Asian and minority ethnic communities. We are deeply concerned that UKRI confirmed that no equality data was collected on this call and that one member of the awards assessment panel is co-investigator on three of the six successfully awarded studies.

Like many other Black individuals involved in research, several of us are precariously employed. According to HESA data, only 1.3 per cent of full-time research positions in the UK are awarded to Black and mixed heritage women, highlighting systemic issues that result in lack of inclusion and persistent precarious employment in higher education.

This year, we have seen our communities disproportionately affected by COVID-19, as this pandemic has illuminated many aspects of systemic and structural discrimination in the UK. We had hoped that this crucial research call would include a wide range of individuals and experts to explore the complex biological, social, cultural and political factors that are connected to the disproportionate impact of COVID-19 on our community. (From an open letter to UKRIs funding allocations during the onset of the COVID-19 pandemic, Adelaine et al, 2020)

Change domains

Diversifying grant makers

Research funders and grant makers need to ensure that their calls for funding and grant making are developed in participatory consultation with Black, Asian and ethnic minority staff that are equipped to critically feed back on meaningful impact on equality and diversity through the lens of intersectionality (that is, centring the voices of those marginalised and deprived at the intersections of gender, race, class, disability, d/Deafness and so on). Consideration of the informal processes of how marginalised Black, Asian and minority ethnic staff are meaningfully involved in the development and success of a grant should be highlighted in funding calls.

Panels for awards

Awarding panels should demonstrate diversity within the panel and clearly articulate conflicts of interest to avoid and deter selection biases. Panels should represent a range of intersecting identities and marginalised groups. If panels are unable to recruit and retain this level of diversity, they should seek sponsorship from Black, Asian and ethnic minority experts and specialist advisors to maintain high quality and rigour in the awarding process. Such advisors should be compensated for their expertise and labour where appropriate.

Transparency in funding data

Transparency of equalities data of applicants and success or reflections for awards should be made available to the public to ensure that any awards can be scrutinised and that large funding institutions are holding themselves to account for meaningful and rational decision making. This data can be sensibly anonymised; however, large funding organisations need to demonstrate to the general public how funds are being allocated, and where there are disparities what these organisations are doing to diversify their funding and research portfolios.

Systemic support for Black and non-Black applicants of colour

Grant makers and research funders need to be including bespoke systems of support to ensure that those racialised as Black and non-Black applicants of colour that are successful in winning a research grant are enabled fair access to the same opportunities White applicants are privileged to receive when they are awarded a research grant. These systems could be related to supporting Black, Asian and minority ethnic staff publication records, line manager support and involvement in research funding applications, and/or developing skills and confidence in grant panel interviews. Funders should embed positive action statements in their calls to further diversify their research and innovation portfolios.

Intersectional contracting

The contracts that are designed and used to underpin research grants need to be considered through the lens of intersectionality; this means considering opportunities and contracting to ensure that those facing multiple disadvantages (for example, Black women living with a disability) are considered and supported in grant and research contracts. Ensuring that safeguards are in place for Black, Asian and minority ethnic applicants, who will be affected by varying levels of racism in that grant, is critical to ethical contracting. It is also advisable to endorse fair access and involvement of Black, Asian and minority ethnic staff in large bids and grants.

Reflective questions

- How are you supporting Black and non-Black applicants of colour to increase their chances of success for a research/grant bid?
- How are you involving Black, Asian and minority ethnic women and wider staff in larger grants and bids?
- What funding are you offering specifically for Black, Asian and minority ethnic applicants?
- How will you support Black, Asian and minority ethnic colleagues who are writing their research grant applications?
- What community of practice can be developed for Black, Asian and minority ethnic teaching/research staff to learn from others' experiences in applying for research funding?
- How do your contracts for research awards protect Black, Asian and minority ethnic applicants from harm?
- Are the contract indicators enablers or barriers to Black, Asian and minority ethnic applicants fulfilling the requirements of the research grant?
- How many experiences as a Black, Asian and minority ethnic student have you had to apply for small research grants?
- What can the institution do to help in applying for smaller research grants during your undergraduate/postgraduate journeys?

References

Adelaine, A., Kalinga, C., Asani, F., Agbakoba, R., Smith, N., Adisa, O., Francois, J., King-Okoye, M., Williams, P. & Zelzer, R. (2020). Knowledge is power – an open letter to UKRI. Accessed 26 September 2020, from www.researchprofessionalnews.com/rr-news-uk-views-of-the-uk-2020-8-knowledge-is-power-an-open-letter-to-ukri/

Brown, K. S., Kijakazi, K., Runes, C. & Turner, M. A. (2019) *Confronting Structural Racism in Research and Policy Analysis.* Washington, DC: Urban Institute. Accessed 1 November 2021, from www.urban.org/sites/default/files/publication/99852/confronting_structural_racism_in_research_and_policy_analysis_0.pdf

Inge, S. (2020) UKRI in row over absence of black PIs in its Covid-19 Black, Asian and minority ethnic grant. Accessed 1 March 2021, from www.researchprofessionalnews.com/rr-news-uk-research-councils-2020-8-ukri-in-row-over-absence-of-black-pis-in-its-covid-19-Black, Asian and minority ethnic-grant/

Li, Y. L., Bretscher, H., Oliver, R. & Ochu, E. (2021) Racism, equity and inclusion in research funding. Accessed 1 March 2021, from https://doi.org/10.31219/osf.io/pgv3x

Murugesu, J. (2019) Ethnic minority academics get less UK research funding. Accessed 26 September 2020, from www.newscientist.com/article/2222994ethnic-minority-academics-get-less-uk-research-funding/

Murugesu, J. & Vaughan, A. (2020) Science's institutional racism. *New Scientist*, 246(3288), 4–15. Accessed 14 October 2021, from www.sciencedirect.com/science/article/abs/pii/S0262407920311258

Ramnani, N. (2022) Diversity in STEM Inquiry. UK Parliament. Accessed 19 February 2022, from https://committees.parliament.uk/writtenevidence/43140/pdf/

Science and Technology Committee (2019) 'My Science Inquiry'. Accessed 12 August 2020, from https://publications.parliament.uk/pa/cm201719/cmselect/cmsctech/1716/171603.htm

Wilkins, S., Neri, S. & Lean, J. (2019) The role of theory in the business/management PhD: how students may use theory to make an original contribution to knowledge. *The International Journal of Management Education*, 17(3), 100316.

8

Research excellence assessments

Arun Verma

Introduction

The notion of research excellence, research awards and the research excellence framework (REF) are significant contributors to disempowering Black, Asian and minority ethnic staff from progressing in their research careers in academia (Rees, 2020). The notion of research excellence is noted to 'typically promote destructive hyper-competition, toxic power dynamics and poor leadership behaviour' (Obasi, 2020). The REF's 2021 equality impact assessment highlighted that more needed to be done to include ethnic minority groups into the process (Reid, 2020). However, the impact assessment makes no mention of intersectionality, or the experience of female Black African and/or Black Caribbean staff that are highly under-represented in academia and in the realm of research excellence. Despite REF panellists who

> receive equality and diversity training and [where] outputs will be analysed by protected characteristics, these post-hoc analyses will not influence university scores. Narrative submissions describing strategies and approaches to support institutional equality and diversity will be assessed under 'environment', but there is no requirement for data about how minorities experience those environments. This is

disappointing, as the presence of strategies has been shown to correlate poorly with actual working conditions and progression for women and minorities in universities. (Obasi, 2020, p 652)

The REF process and experience is at the heart of perpetuating systemic racism, prohibiting Black and ethnic minority academics' progress in their research careers where such marginalisation disempowers and disables Black, Asian and minority ethnic researchers' voices, presence and experience (Mirza, 2018).

Voices from literature

On its website in March 2017, HEFCE noted that the previous equality and diversity panel had 'expressed disappointment' that limited progress had been made since the 2008 Research Assessment Exercise towards increasing diversity in the membership of the REF panel, which judges the ratings that research submissions are awarded.

The backdrop to HEFCE's decision is a growing body of evidence that suggests that racism persists in higher education despite significant advances in policy making and student body diversity. Recent statistics indicate that Black and minority ethnic staff remain and that they are far less likely to become professors compared to their White colleagues.

HEFCE found evidence to show that Black and Asian UK staff were less likely to be selected for inclusion in the REF 2014 exercise compared to White staff. The University and College Union has argued that one in 10 Black and minority ethnic (BME) academics regarded their institutions' REF selection as discriminatory based on race.

It is too easy to employ a rhetoric of inclusion, while failing to deliver substantive outcomes. This is particularly problematic when there remains evidence of persistent and deep-rooted inequalities based on race. (Extract from Bhopal, 2017)

Change domains

Prioritising research integrity, dignity and respect

The redefining of research excellence must be tied with research integrity through the lens of anti-racism. It needs to address and ensure its function, purpose and scope is fair, equitable and diverse. Anti-racist research integrity frameworks are a crucial mechanism to ensure that research excellence is premised on impact, accountability and participatory action, and are supported by recent evidence calling for research integrity to drive diversity and inclusion (for example, DuBois & Antes, 2018; Shaw & Satalkar, 2018; Moher et al, 2020).

Reforming the research excellence framework

The REF needs to consider how it can be redesigned and co-created to involve, engage and include Black, Asian and minority ethnic academics to have the same opportunities and access to successfully performing in REF reviews meaningfully and authentically. In McKie's (2019) article, Professor Neylon refers to the REF as perpetuating a neo-colonial agenda, and international partnerships and collaborations, and the notion of research excellence needs to be considered through both globally transferable and localisation approaches to ensure we reimagine research excellence in the UK HE sector. Localisation can be a key tool in ensuring that research excellence is measured and evaluated concerning how local agendas in collaborative research programmes reflect and adopt a more intercultural approach to research excellence.

> interpersonal and critical cross-cultural engagement … [this is] not only as a political mechanism at the global sphere but also as a policy strategy to manage people-to-people relations in diverse settings. This vertical shift allows [localisation approaches] to contribute proactively to social cohesion agendas in diversity settings (at the local level). Furthermore, and in changing its sphere of application (from global to local) and public objective (from states and

regions to people and migrants). (Zapata-Barrero & Mansouri, 2021)

When reflecting on internationally leading research, an intercultural framework for change could still support a scale of international excellence retaining a global globally sensitive lens, while supporting local infrastructures and agency of international partners (Zapata-Barrero & Mansouri, 2021).

Anti-racism training and learning

Research excellence and funding panels must undergo mandatory robust anti-racism training prior to becoming a panellist to ensure racial aggressions are not enacted in the review process. This is particularly required to ensure that where panels are not diverse, they are able to provide standardised feedback and comments based on a co-created framework and criteria for scoring research excellence submissions. It also ensures that panellists, who are typically leaders in specialist fields across the HE sector, are continuing and building their knowledge in areas of race equity and equality, while reducing prejudice, discrimination and racial harassment both in the REF framework and more widely across HE (Ben, Kelly & Paradies, 2020).

Research excellence transparency

The REF requires transparency in its process and decision making to ensure high levels of accountability with more public facing and accountable decision making to be made known to wider communities (O'Regan & Gray, 2018). Processes and policies associated with the REF can be hidden and discreet, making it difficult to ascertain what decisions are made, and how, when and under what circumstances (O'Regan & Gray, 2018). Mechanisms for transparency can be as simple as noting equalities data for submissions in relation to award outcomes, transparency in decision-making processes, transparency in what and how equalities training is delivered to panellists along with how that is moderated. Further consideration of how civic and public engagement is enabled and how these scores are rationalised in international and collaborative applications is required.

Reflective questions

- Are you able to fully appreciate how Black, Asian and minority ethnic researchers will have reduced opportunities and access to engaging with the REF?
- How will you ensure that the support of Black, Asian and minority ethnic panellists remains in place for all REFs?
- How will you involve Black and ethnic minority staff and students in the REF's continuous improvement, design and implementation process?
- How as a research group and staff are you empowering Black and ethnic minority academics to achieve local, national and international research excellence in your department and institution?
- How are you ensuring that Black, Asian and minority ethnic staff are supported in generating and developing a strong research publication and grant portfolio to further their success in prospective REF submissions?
- How is the management and operations of the REF conducted in a way that includes Black and ethnic minority panellists and nominees?

References

Ben, J., Kelly, D. & Paradies, Y. (2020) Contemporary anti-racism: a review of effective practice. In *International Handbook of Contemporary Racisms* (pp 205–15). London: Routledge.

Bhopal, K. (2017) A nearly all-white diversity panel? When will universities start taking race seriously? *The Guardian*. Accessed 26 August 2020, from www.theguardian.com/higher-education-network/2017/may/31/a-clash-of-personalities-why-universities-mustnt-ignore-race

DuBois, J. M. & Antes, A. L. (2018) Five dimensions of research ethics: a stakeholder framework for creating a climate of research integrity. *Academic Medicine: Journal of the Association of American Medical Colleges*, 93(4), 550.

McKie, A. (2019) REF must 'bring hammer down' on open access books, says professor. *Times Higher Education*. Accessed 19 August 2022, from www.timeshighereducation.com/news/ref-must-bring-hammer-down-open-access-books-says-professor

Mirza, H. S. (2018) Racism in higher education: 'What then, can be done?'. In *Dismantling Race in Higher Education* (pp 3–23). Cham: Palgrave Macmillan.

Moher, D., Bouter, L., Kleinert, S., Glasziou, P., Sham, M. H., Barbour, V., Coriat, A. M., Foeger, N. & Dirnagl, U. (2020) The Hong Kong principles for assessing researchers: fostering research integrity. *PLoS Biology*, 18(7), e3000737.

Obasi, A. I. (2020) Equity in excellence or just another tax on black skin? *Lancet*, 396(10252), 651–653. DOI: 10.1016/S0140-6736(20)31536-1.

O'Regan, J. P. & Gray, J. (2018) The bureaucratic distortion of academic work: a transdisciplinary analysis of the UK Research Excellence Framework in the age of neoliberalism. *Language and Intercultural Communication*, 18(5), 533–48.

Rees, J. (2020) Race, racism and social policy. *Social Policy Review 32: Analysis and Debate in Social Policy*. Cambridge: Cambridge University Press.

Reid, G. (2020) Equality Impact Assessment for the Research Excellence Framework 2021. Accessed 26 August 2020, from www.ref.ac.uk/media/1315/ref-eia-updated-march-2020.pdf

Shaw, D. & Satalkar, P. (2018) Researchers' interpretations of research integrity: a qualitative study. *Accountability in Research*, 25(2), 79–93.

Zapata-Barrero, R. & Mansouri, F. (2021) A multi-scale approach to interculturalism: from globalised politics to localised policy and practice. *Journal of International Migration and Integration*, 1–21. DOI: 10.1007/s12134-021-00846-w.

9

Research collaborations and publishing

Arun Verma

Introduction

National and international research partnerships are often created by senior staff through tokenism and nepotism, which is highlighted when it comes to topics of authorship and peer review (Sandström & Hällsten, 2007; Silva et al, 2019). With the rise of international collaborations as an indicator of research excellence, there is still little attention paid to the continuous inclusion of Black, Asian and minority ethnic academics in the context of research collaborations (Parker & Kingori, 2016). Parker and Kingori also highlight that such collaborations can be a deterrent for Black, Asian and minority ethnic academics, as they can be perceived as tokenistic and knowing that they will be subject to racist behaviours in their role.

Peer review and authorship play a significant role in perpetuating systemic racism and 'raises still broader issues of racial discrimination against Black [people] and other minority faculty members in the academic labour market generally' (Coleman, 2005, p 763). In one example it is noted that

> articles in psychological journals that highlight race have been rare, and although developmental and social psychology journals have published

> a growing number of these articles, they have remained virtually non-existent in cognitive psychology ... most journals have been edited by White editors, under whom there has been a notable dearth of published articles highlighting race and racism ... many of the publications that highlight race have been written by White authors, who employed significantly fewer participants of colour. (Psychological Science, 2020)

There is a critical issue in the belonging and inclusion of Black, Asian and minority ethnic researchers and successful research collaborations, partnerships and publishing in HE, reflected by racial harassment and exclusion, and these are considered further in the 'Voices from literature' section.

Voices from literature

> things ... have to be kind of acknowledged by both sides and trust and talked about in a very, very open way and I don't think is something that is ever discussed really, really between partners ... it's one of those things that you think oh it's better not to go there because it's just going to come across as being patronising or racist or whatever so let's not address the fact that there's a disparity in the capacity or there's a disparity in terms of contribution let's just concentrate on what it is that we're going to do. (Parker & Kingori, 2016, p 11)

> Actually not that much has changed ... the relationship between the North and the South is still exactly as it was, the North has money and tries to dictate the research agenda. Africans are continually trying to respond to somebody else's agenda whilst having their own agenda at the same time which I think very often doesn't get investigated (European Principal Investigator, East Africa). (Parker & Kingori, 2016, p 10)

Change domains

Diversifying editors of mainstream journals

Currently, the editorial boards of mainstream journals do not represent the range of participants who researchers collect data from or with. Editorial boards of academic publishers need to reconsider meaningful race and marginalised intersectional representation to ensure that publishers, editors and reviewers are reviewing submissions in a fair manner, and challenge a White gaze, saviourism and privilege in academic journal editing. Utilising quantitative and qualitative positive action can accelerate this diversity on editorial boards.

Challenging authorship, peer review and nepotism

Racial bias in academic publishing is continually reported on, with explicit reports of the White Bull whose 'profile [is] of a type of serial abuser ... who uses his academic seniority to distort authorship credit and who disguises his parasitism with carefully premeditated deception' (Kwok, 2005, p 554). Additionally, examples of racially motivated nepotism have been recorded and noted in the example here, of the

> devaluation of a [Black, Asian and minority ethnic staff's] capacities both on initial entry to the British education system and in employment, compared to [another's] experience of 'progress through the sponsorship of senior White men'. There were no sponsors for [the staff member] and nobody to guide him on the 'publish or perish' rules of his department which rewarded research activity with promotion. (Mahoney & Weiner, 2019, p 854–5)

Challenging racially biased nepotism and tokenism in peer review and authorship can start to shift cultures, knowledge production and equity, ensuring that authorship stretches beyond the White inner circles of academia and embraces Black, Asian and ethnic minority academics and cultures.

Valuing Black, Asian and minority ethnic staff contribution to collaborations

The value of Black, Asian and minority ethnic staff contributions to collaborations is undervalued by White staff, which is often combined with ethnic minority staff perceived as being less competent (Sian, 2017). Creating a culture of appreciation, value and strength to ensure that the expertise that Black, Asian and minority ethnic staff bring is recognised needs to be embedded in research collaborations that require a cultural shift to challenge 'White Bulls' that are noted to lead these networks (Kwok, 2005).

Reflective questions

- 'Why are Black faculty members concentrated at the lowest academic ranks and least prestigious academic institutions?' (Coleman, 2005)
- 'How could scientific racism elude an editor and peer reviewers at a prestigious journal?' (Coleman, 2005)
- 'How could a White [expert] ignore [their] own evidence that the publishing system is biased, inasmuch as non-Black scholars do not have to deal with non-mainstream publishing?' (Coleman, 2005)
- How are you ensuring that research collaborations and authorship meaningfully include Black, Asian and minority ethnic staff to ensure they have the same opportunities as those who are White?
- How are you challenging imperial authorship norms to be more inclusive and recognise author contributions?
- How will you ensure that you will avoid colonising international collaborators from the Global East and South?
- How does your research and innovation systems enable Black, Asian and minority ethnic staff to thrive in forming and maintaining research collaborations?
- Do the mechanisms that house such collaborations include anti-racism thinking and guidance?

References

Coleman, M. G. (2005) Racism in academia: the white superiority supposition in the 'unbiased' search for knowledge. *European Journal of Political Economy*, 21(3), 762–74. DOI: 10.1016/j.ejpoleco.2004.08.004.

Da Silva, J. A. T., Katavić, V., Dobránszki, J., Al-Khatib, A. & Bornemann-Cimenti, H. (2019) Establishing rules for ethicists and ethics organizations in academic publishing to avoid conflicts of interest, favoritism, cronyism and nepotism. *KOME*, 7(1), 110–125. DOI: 10.17646/kome.75698.87.

Kwok, L. S. (2005) The White Bull effect: abusive co-authorship and publication parasitism. *Journal of Medical Ethics*, 31(9), 554. DOI: 10.1136/jme.2004.010553.

Mahony, P. & Weiner, G. (2019) 'Getting in, getting on, getting out': Black, Asian and minority ethnic staff in UK higher education. *Race Ethnicity and Education*, 23(6), 1–17. DOI: 10.1080/13613324.2019.1679761.

Parker, M. & Kingori, P. (2016) Good and bad research collaborations: researchers' views on science and ethics in global health research. *PloS One*, 11(10), e0163579.

Psychological Science. (2020) Psychological research: racial biases in the peer-review and publishing enterprise – association for psychological science – APS. *Psychological Science*. Accessed 1 August 2021, from www.psychologicalscience.org/publications/observer/obsonline/racial-biases-in-publications.html

Sandström, U. & Hällsten, M. (2007) Persistent nepotism in peer-review. *Scientometrics*, 74(2), 175–89. DOI: 10.1007/s11192-008-0211-3.

Sian, K. (2017) 'Being black in a white world: understanding racism in british universities'. *International Journal on Collective Identity Research*, 2017(2), 1–26.

PART V

Teaching systems enabling racism

10

Teaching and scholarship funding, contracts and collaboration

Arun Verma

Introduction

Funding for developing teaching and scholarship staff and teaching fellows is a critical issue for Black, Asian and minority ethnic staff who are affected by poor quality of working life and less success in gaining teaching awards to develop their careers (Hey et al, 2011). Teaching contracts can often be amended to inhibit staff in pursuing meaningful professional and faculty development opportunities and effective teaching partnerships, which are the essence of advancing scholarship, student experience and outcomes (Borah, Malik & Massini, 2021). With the rising number of teaching and scholarship and teaching fellowships in universities, these scholarly partnerships enable universities to advance their widening access and internationalisation strategies. Teaching contracts, funding and collaboration are intrinsically linked, and it is Black and ethnic minority HE teaching staff that are most marginalised in their contract and teaching experiences (Brewis, 2019). Findings have highlighted how HE teaching and scholarship staff of colour will experience invisibility, vulnerability, a lack of agency and inability to see their future career progression (Megoran & Mason, 2020). It has also been highlighted that Black, Asian and minority ethnic identifying HE teachers face obstacles to promotions and career progression. Teachers have 'spoken of the way in which racism manifested itself through hidden White networks' (Sian, 2019) that excluded them from various opportunities. One participant called this a 'perpetuating machine' in which White colleagues 'co-sign each other's applications, share each other's teaching content, and support one another' (Sian, 2019). These racisms inhibit and continue to disable Black, Asian and minority ethnic academic teaching staff to progress their careers, secure fellowships and negotiate their teaching contracts.

Voices from literature

As a Black, Asian and minority ethnic lecturer at UAL it is very isolating. I've been lecturing there for 11 years – 6 on an MA course. I am in the same role on paper that I was when I became 'staff' on the course but am often paid several months late. I am not very visible in my role, as I am helicoptered in. I realized when we went online that evening though I am always involved in assessments and marking I am probably not even noted down as a marker in the system (I only saw because my line manager shared his screen with the marking going online as he didn't realise that part was visible). In a workshop about Diversity and Black, Asian and minority ethnic attainment sitting in the room with colleagues as the speaker stated: "we as White lecturers …" I was sitting right in front of her! Not only was it an assumption but she couldn't even bother to change the narrative or her script when confronting a different reality. [Shaking my damn head] … being introduced by the course director to the creative director of a large luxury brand that our course was working with on a student design project "This is X, someone we work with". That was it, no title, no context. I have been working as an AL on the course for 6 years and in other documentation, when it suits, am described as a 'key academic' on the course. … I'll just put two down for now because to be honest I could write a book. (UAL Truth, 2020)[1]

I said to the head of department "I'm not putting up with it. I've never been spoken to in the way I've been spoken to by him, and I want an apology" and the Head of Department was very good … and … [he] spoke to him and he had to come and give me an apology. However, lack of follow-up resulted in Nora becoming … a marked woman. He just then had it in for me, picked on me, bullied. It was just awful, I was so relieved when he stopped, when he left. Little digs all the time. He was awful, really, really bad. (Mahony & Weiner, 2019, p 849)

Change domains

The following change areas provide critical opportunities for embedding equality and fairness in a part of the university system that is crucial to staff and student experience.

Systemic support for teaching and scholarship staff

Ensure that policies and procedures are in place to safeguard and support Black, Asian and minority ethnic staff who are prohibited from engaging in teaching and scholarship activities to progress their careers and chances of securing teaching grants and fellowships for their development and institutional excellence. This is particularly pertinent to ensure that teaching and scholarship contracts are culturally, racially and intersectionally sensitive, that they do not create barriers but dismantle them for academic staff in these roles.

Protecting time

Provide opportunities for Black, Asian and minority ethnic teaching staff to negotiate protected time in their contracts to ensure that they can dedicate time to securing grants and providing exceptional teaching, learning and student experiences in the institutions. Staff are increasingly expected not only to publish scholarship in their area of teaching, but also to be applying and winning teaching and scholarship awards, while teaching often large cohorts of students, which can often result in high workloads for early-career teaching staff. Providing flexibility in contracts for staff to choose how they use their own protected time can enable autonomy and some academic freedom, while being mindful of institutional and academic commitments.

Teaching spaces and places

Ensure that spaces for teaching staff are actively addressing explicitly colonialism to ensure Black, Asian and minority ethnic identifying staff can assimilate and have a sense of belonging in different institutional spaces and places. Such spaces can make Black, Asian and minority ethnic teaching staff feel secondary, othered and misplaced in spaces. Actively increasing the diversity of such spaces using physical and social cues could enable a more dignified and respectful teaching and learning space for staff and students (for example, Maringe, 2017).

Enabling Black, Asian and minority ethnic colleagues

Encourage and enable White teaching staff to embrace and empower Black, Asian and minority ethnic teaching staff in their communities of practice to ensure teaching staff are sharing and involving Black, Asian and minority ethnic staff in developing best practices in their institutions. White teaching staff hold a privilege and platform that can be used to further EEDI across HE teaching and learning spaces and to embed anti-racism. Working to support and empower marginalised and deprived staff can create more successful working environments for departments, schools, faculties/colleges and for the wider institution.

Reflective questions

- Do all your Black, Asian and minority ethnic teaching staff have contracts that protect their time for developing best teaching scholarship, practice and research?

- Are your Black, Asian and minority ethnic teaching staff able to negotiate and/or challenge their contracts in a safe way to ensure they are able to have access to continuing professional development in their department?
- Have you ensured that there is a culture that supports Black, Asian and minority ethnic staff to assimilate into White networks and spaces in your department/institution?
- How are you supporting Black, Asian and minority ethnic academic and professional staff to be engaged and involved in supporting and developing learning technologies?
- How as a student and group are you providing constructive feedback to Black, Asian and minority ethnic teaching staff in your course evaluations?

Note
[1] www.instagram.com/ualtruth/?hl=en

References

Arday, J. & Mirza, H. S. (eds) (2018) *Dismantling Race in Higher Education: Racism, Whiteness and Decolonising the Academy.* Cham: Springer.

Borah, D., Malik, K. & Massini, S. (2021) Teaching-focused university–industry collaborations: determinants and impact on graduates' employability competencies. *Research Policy*, 50(3), 104172.

Brewis, D. (2019) Building the anti-racist classroom. Accessed 26 August 2020, from https://wonkhe.com/blogs/building-the-anti-racist-classroom/

Hey, V., Dunne, M., Aynsley, S., Kimura, M., Bennion, A., Brennan, J. & Patel, J. (2011) The experience of black and minority ethnic staff in higher education in England. Accessed 30 December 2020, from www.ecu.ac.uk/wp-content/uploads/external/experience-of-bme-staff-in-he-final-report.pdf

Mahony, P. & Weiner, G. (2019) 'Getting in, getting on, getting out': black, Asian and minority ethnic staff in UK higher education. *Race Ethnicity and Education*, 2023(6), 1–17.

Maringe, F. (2017) Creating opportunities for a socially just pedagogy: the imperatives of transformation in post-colonial HE spaces. In *Transforming Teaching and Learning in Higher Education* (pp 59–78). Cham: Palgrave Macmillan.

Megoran, N. & Mason, O. (2020) UCU. Accessed 26 August 2020, from www.ucu.org.uk/media/10681/second_class_academic_citizens/pdf/secondclassacademiccitizens

Sian, K. (2019) Racism in UK universities is blocking black, Asian and minority ethnic academics from the top. *The Guardian.* Accessed 27 August 2020, from www.theguardian.com/education/2019/jul/10/racism-in-uk-universities-is-blocking-Black, Asian and minority ethnic-academics-from-the-top

UAL Truth [@ualtruth] (2020) BIPOC staff @unioftheartslondon paid several months late!!! Are not acknowledged for their roles or positions and are disrespected by other white staff #ual #ualstillsowhite #ualisracist [Photograph]. *Instagram.* Accessed 1 February 2021, from https://www.instagram.com/p/CB6XMpRFufO/

11

Teaching excellence assessments

Arun Verma

Introduction

The introduction of teaching excellence, teaching awards and the teaching excellence framework (TEF) can be counterproductive to creating a thriving teaching culture for Black, Asian and minority ethnic staff in progressing their teaching careers in academia, particularly with a focus on HE as a market and a form of consumerism that can lose sight of critical discussions concerning pedagogy, learning and teaching theory (Tomlinson et al, 2020). It is this current notion of teaching excellence that is embedded within the racist and White supremacies identified in the ideas of research excellence (Obasi, 2020).

The TEF 'is a national exercise, introduced by the government in England. It assesses excellence in teaching at universities and colleges, and how each higher education provider ensures excellent outcomes for their students in terms of graduate-level employment or further study' (Office for Students, 2020). It is mostly informed by the National Student Survey (NSS), and upon its implementation was considered to perpetuate inequalities in students' access and retention in HE (French, 2020). It is noted that 'splitting university performance on the core metrics based on NSS scores by student "domicile" (United Kingdom, EU, and non-EU), as it is currently proposed in the plans for the TEF, is not sufficient. The rationale behind such "splitting" is to incentivise universities to address inequity among different student groups' (Hayes, 2017). It is also evidenced that the NSS, which heavily informs the TEF, finds that students will give lower scores in teaching excellence to Black, Asian and minority ethnic academics (Asquith, 2016). An analysis of NSS survey data from '2014 results found that the ethnicity of lecturers was one of the most significant influencers on the overall satisfaction of UK undergraduates' (Havergal, 2016). However, despite efforts to continuously improve the TEF, the framework continues to neglect to involve the voices of Black, Asian and minority ethnic students and staff in its development and outputs (Cui, 2020).

Lacking a voice

There is currently little literature exploring the role of the teaching excellence framework (TEF) through the lens of race and racial disparities, with some literature highlighting the emphasis on the role student experience plays in recognising teaching excellence (for example, Suki, 2020). In Suki's paper (p 3), they highlight

> the rise of managerialism and in particular, audit cultures, [which] have allowed racism to flourish in spite, or rather because of, the need to account for equality, diversity and inclusion in global markets for higher education. Auditing requires a focus on identities and cannot consider the complex ways in which race, race thinking, and racism are maintained in knowledge production.

However, such arguments and lines of inquiry need to be further interrogated to capture the racial and intersectional disparities that exist and are perpetuated as part of the TEF.

Change domains

Reassessing the teaching excellence framework

Reassessment and redesign of the TEF with a race equality and intersectionality lens will ensure that it is inclusive to Black,

Asian and minority ethnic teaching, scholarship and research staff in universities. A meaningful co-design process in the TEF's continuous improvement will be able to integrate further standardisation of the framework and additionally ensure that diversity and inclusion play a critical role in the mechanics of the TEF. Such assurances will enable Black, Asian and minority ethnic teaching staff to increase their engagement with TEF applications while ensuring such staff are in better positions to progress their careers and support the diversification of their teaching and organisational influence.

Reconsidering the emphasis of the National Student Survey in teaching excellence

Satisfaction is only one measure of excellence in the realm of pedagogy, teaching and learning. While there is appreciation that NSS is critical for universities and regulators to have a sense of the qualities of the HE experience, a more rigorous critical framework that considers excellence as a rubric with diversity and inclusion at its core could facilitate a more meaningful assessment of teaching excellence in furthering a thriving culture for all staff and students. Reimagining the NSS to ensure it further accounts for respondent and interpretative bias can help mitigate against the adversities that Black, Asian and minority ethnic staff and students face when it comes to access, participation, recruitment, retention and success in the HE sector.

Implementing a field on equality, diversity and inclusion

The TEF should consider integrating a section into the assessment concerning questions, metrics and indicators specific to equity and EDI particularly while being mindful of the sensitivities of those who are racially minoritised and live with multiple intersecting disadvantages (for example, gender, class and race). Cultivating and prompting thinking, analysis and evidence in this area could help produce stronger data to inform structural racial disparities that are reflected in the Black and White student degree-awarding gaps, as well as graduate outcomes for students.

Reflective questions

- Are you ensuring and enabling Black, Asian and minority ethnic academics to perform well in the TEF?
- How will you ensure that the support and retention of Black panellists remains in place for all TEF assessments?
- How will you involve Black and ethnic minority staff and students into co-creation and co-design of teaching excellence in your institution?
- How as teaching staff are you empowering Black and ethnic minority academics to achieve teaching excellence in your field?
- How are you encouraging students to address their implicit racial biases when completing the NSS?
- How is the management and operations of the TEF conducted in a way that includes Black and ethnic minority panellists and nominees?
- How are you as students ensuring you recognise your implicit racial biases before completing the NSS?

References

Asquith, S. (2016) Institutional racism, marketization and the national student survey. Accessed 27 August 2020, from https://network23.org/freeunisheff/2016/02/01/racism-marketization-the-nss/

Cui, V. (2020) A missed opportunity? How the UK's teaching excellence framework fails to capture the voice of university staff. Accessed 30 December 2020, from https://blogs.lse.ac.uk/impactofsocialsciences/2020/04/28/a-missed-opportunity-how-the-uks-teaching-excellence-framework-fails-to-capture-the-voice-of-university-staff/

French, A. (2020) 'It's not what gets taught, or how well it may be taught, but who is doing the teaching': can student evaluations ever deliver a fair assessment on teaching excellence in higher education? In *Challenging the Teaching Excellence Framework* (pp 151–178). Bingley: Emerald Publishing Limited.

Havergal, C. (2016) 'Biased' students give BME academics lower NSS scores, says study. Accessed 27 August 2020, from www.timeshighereducation.com/news/biased-students-give-bme-academics-lower-nss-scores-says-study

Hayes, A. (2017) The teaching excellence framework in the United Kingdom: an opportunity to include international students as 'equals'? *Journal of Studies in International Education*, 21(5), 483–97. DOI: 10.1177/1028315317720768.

Obasi, A. I. (2020) Equity in excellence or just another tax on black skin? *Lancet*, 396(10252), 651–653. DOI: 10.1016/S0140-6736(20)31536-1.

Office for Students (2020) About the TEF – Office for Students. Accessed 27 August 2020, from www.officeforstudents.org.uk/advice-and-guidance/teaching/about-the-tef/

Suki, A. (2020) Managing racism? Race equality and decolonial educational futures. working paper (47). International Inequalities Institute, London School of Economics and Political Science, London, UK.

Tomlinson, M., Enders, J. & Naidoo, R. (2020) The teaching excellence framework: symbolic violence and the measured market in higher education. *Critical Studies in Education*, 61(5), 627–42.

PART VI

Pedagogies that enable racism

12

Pedagogies, professionalism and curricula enabling racism

Musharrat J. Ahmed-Landeryou

Introduction

In searching for research regarding racist pedagogy in HE, literature continuously deferred to the term antiracist[1] pedagogy. Within relevant papers, racist pedagogy may have an introductory discussion, for example, regarding discriminatory, exclusory or Eurocentric curriculum and consequences see Wagner, 2005; Montgomery, 2013). A rapid scoping evaluation of research literature was carried out into the subject of whether pedagogy/ies in HE is/are perpetuating and/or supporting racism in the curriculum. This was extrapolated from literature related to antiracist pedagogy of curriculum design. EBSCO (Elton Brysons Stephens & Co), an online platform for research databases such as Academic Complete, ERIC (Education Resources Information Centre) and Education Research Complete, were searched for relevant research.

There are key learning needs, education and training of students within the curriculum and staff on culture as an institutional approach, specifically, exploring culture as a tool for learning and to adjust to cultures (Jabbar & Mirza, 2019), cultural awareness (Singh, 2019), culture as a core topic as a levelling technique, promoting equity by both explaining and solving problems (Jeyasingham & Morton, 2019) and staff understanding cultural norms and diversity. Included in these is immersion into issues of power and privilege, through the lens of social justice (Hill et al, 2018).

Disparate learning needs of Black, Asian and Minoritised Ethnic and White students being different regarding racism need to be appreciated and built into the curriculum (Jeyasingham & Morton, 2019; Singh, 2019), and reflected in literature resources and reading lists for courses as there is a tendency for them to be Eurocentric and White male-dominated, as in sciences (Crilly, Panesar & Suka-Bill, 2020; Schucan Bird & Pitman, 2020). Additionally, student feedback says that Black, Asian and Minoritised Ethnic and White students receive and perceive training about race and racism differently (Singh, 2019).

Solutions for change as part of an institutional approach include collaboration between staff and students to co-design and apply antiracist pedagogy to transform the curriculum , for example, diversifying the reading lists (Crilly, Panesar & Suka-Bill, 2020; Schucan Bird & Pitman, 2020); internationalising the curriculum content (Jeyasingham & Morton, 2019); applying a strength-based frame for curriculum that values diversity; and staff to reflect and review how teaching practices construct race, Whiteness [or 'Eurocentricness'] and oppression, to improve the awarding gap (Jabbar & Mirza, 2019; Jeyasingham & Morton, 2019).

In relation to Husbands and Pearce's (2012) nine items for effective pedagogy delivery, the solutions for change relate to five of the items: co-design; integrating what teachers know, want to do and why they act; short and long-term goals; scaffolding; and integrating diverse needs. Current strategies to embed antiracist pedagogy are reduced in their effectiveness when they are not integrated into these items for sustainable change. The literature indicates that the curriculum and underlying pedagogy continues to be racist, because changes to curriculum are still being requested to stop disadvantaging Black, Asian and minority ethnic students (Tate & Bagguley, 2017).

Removing racist pedagogy or implementing meaningful antiracist pedagogy is not an easy fix of just including diverse and racial content in courses and curricula of disciplines. The past attempts of institutions to implement antiracist policies have failed as we are here writing an antiracist action guide for HE. The reason for the failure is offered by Tate and Bagguley (2017), in that past liberal inclusive approaches to embed antiracism have not taken into account the pervasiveness of the Racial Contract (Leonardo, 2013). The Racial Contract intensely continues the protection of the White privilege space of power, which has a strong emotional reaction to protect those it relates to, thus maintaining the oppression and inequality for Black, Asian and Minoritised Ethnic staff and students (Tate & Bagguley, 2017). The Racial Contract sustains the dominance of the Western/ Eurocentric focus of curriculum and hence racist pedagogy (Tate & Bagguley, 2017).

Epistemic exploitation is an additional coercive and exploitative labour for Black, Asian and Minoritised Ethnic populations to educate their oppressors regarding how they are oppressing (Berenstain, 2016). This labour is time-consuming, emotionally harrowing and not remunerated, the latter really emphasising the imbalance of power (Berenstain, 2016). Hence, all this leads to the shift to equity being short-lived or not felt at all. This space has to be disrupted for real meaningful actions for change to take root and lead to positive progress. It requires a whole institutional approach for antiracist transformative change, to enable antiracist pedagogy to reach and land across the HE hierarchy, through meaningful actions for the betterment of all students, and furthermore contributing to social change (Kishimoto, 2018). Within this transformational framework is incorporated the political character of HE and racialisation, and the dynamic interrelationships of knowledge, cultures and systems of power (SOAS, 2018). This acknowledgement of White privilege, power structures and processes through transparent and uncomfortable discussions and strategic planning to action meaningful antiracist change will break the stronghold of the Racial Contract and remove the continuance of epistemic exploitation.

'When racism is understood only as individual prejudice, racism embedded in institutions is ignored. At the same time, focusing only on institutional racism allows individuals benefiting from racism to avoid any responsibility' (Kishimoto, 2018, p 542).

Voice of the author

From my observations, politically and policy-wise, race and racism are continually left out of the discussions to implement meaningful actions, and to monitor and review outcome measures and persistence in collaboration with all stakeholders. The continuous quest for more reviews and consultations only makes the people in the White privilege power base feel better and stay in power, and keeps opening up and laying bare the historical scars and noxious consequences of inaction. James Baldwin timelessly said, "as a negro to be conscious is to be in rage all the time" because everywhere the system is disadvantaging most Black, Asian and Minoritised Ethnic persons. It is not about creating a colour-blind society or institution, or even about allyship. It is about making authentic antiracist actions that are deep-seated in the institutions of power, because in the end this benefits all in society. So, in HE there must be no more gestures of tokenism, for now is the time to wholeheartedly embrace social justice in education through actioning antiracist pedagogy. Start right, start somewhere, and it will go everywhere.

Change domains

Rethinking leadership

This is based on the National Education Union (2019, p 9) framework for schools developing a whole institutional antiracist approach, ensuring that leadership models are invested in commitment to antiracist values and a whole school/college approach to race equality. Leadership should be considered as an opportunity to challenge race inequality, achieve cultural inclusion and respond to the differences in students' lives caused by racism, poverty and discrimination. HE institutions must centrally put in place infrastructure, policies and resources to commit to being antiracist and offer diversity and internationalising, not Western/Eurocentric, curriculum content. Institutions can explicate their position as being an antiracist campus and this could be embedded in the institutional vision statement, in its working philosophy, in its workforce and how it supports its Black, Asian and Minoritised Ethnic staff and students. Policies and procedures for staff and students must explicitly enable a racism-free safe zone. Reported issues of racism must be recorded and the meaningful learning, actions and outcomes documented.

In HE, embedding antiracist pedagogy will require recognition of alternative perspectives in the analysis of privilege and White power relations, including race, gender and class. This shows authenticity, transparency and commitment to being an antiracist university with antiracist curricula. Review and monitor annually through student and staff feedback, and record and share action changes.

Effective pedagogy in race equality

Husbands and Pearce's (2012) nine items of effective pedagogy should be integrated in the whole institution strategy to deliver antiracist pedagogy in the curriculum. The schools/faculties should have to explicitly take the antiracist position, which is evident in all their materials from promo to teaching delivery and content and learning materials. Monitor and review the curriculum against Husbands and Pearce's (2012) antiracist education institution framework and its nine items, and record and share action changes.

Diversifying content, reading and literature

Diversify and internationalise the reading lists, reducing the Western-centric and White male author overrepresentation, and co-produce with students. Review and monitor annually through student and staff feedback. Key learning regarding racism should be built into all modules in the curricula, integrated with the different learning needs and outcomes, and teaching methods for the Black, Asian and Minoritised Ethnic and White students, assuring that the classroom is a safe space. Annually monitor and review the curriculum against Husbands and Pearce's (2012) antiracist education institution framework and its nine items, and record and share action changes.

All modules in courses should include race, inequality and colonialism in subjects to enable explicit understanding and discussion and reduce Western/Eurocentric concept/topic dominance. This will go towards improving the empowerment of Black, Asian and Minoritised Ethnic students in White spaces and promoting the active adjacency positioning of White students against racism. Evaluate, monitor and review from student feedback; record and demonstrate transparency and accountability in the delivery of actions and changes.

Equity and equality impact reviews of modules

Annual reflection and reviewing of modules by staff to recheck the positional stance of modules in relation to antiracism should occur, and data should be collected to demonstrate the impact of change due to antiracist pedagogy; for example, student satisfaction, pass rates and staff diversity could be separated into ethnicities for comparing with previous years.

To critically develop antiracist pedagogy ask and answer reflective questions

- How do you measure that you are promoting an antiracist organisation and that it is culturally intelligent?
- Whose voices are heard in your institution?
- Do Black staff feel valued and safe?
- Do Black parents feel valued and respected in school/college?
- With regards to wellbeing and belonging, which students feel a sense of belonging? Why?
- Is student wellbeing seen as a priority?
- What are the links between racism and wellbeing in your institution?
- When thinking about community, what is the local history in your area? How can you use it to discuss protests, struggles or campaigns led by Black communities in your area?
- What antiracist pedagogical strategies are you using?
- Is your curriculum predominantly White, Western, Eurocentric or ethnically neutral?
- Is your service culturally intelligent?
- Do you engage in or feel able to discuss race or racism in the classroom environment in relation to classroom dynamics and/

or placement environment and/or learning materials and/or study skills support?

Note

1 The author deliberately uses the term antiracism/ist without the hyphen to consolidate and bring together anti and racism as an activist word form and neologism.

References

Berenstain, N. (2016) Epistemic exploitation, ergo an open access. *Journal of Philosophy*, 3(22), 569–90.

Bhopal, K. & Pitkin, C. (2018) *Investigating Higher Education Institutions and their Views on the Race Equality Charter*, London: UCU. Accessed 24 July 2020, from www.ucu.org.uk/media/9526/Investigating-higher-education-institutions-and-their-views-on-the-Race-Equality-Charter/pdf/Race_Equality_Charter_Kalwant_Bhopal_Clare_Pitkin.pdf

Crilly, J., Panesar, L. & Suka-Bill, Z. (2020) Co-constructing a liberated/decolonised arts curriculum. *Journal of University Teaching & Learning Practice*, 17(2), 1–16.

DaCunha, J. & Cidalia, M. (2016) Disrupting Eurocentric education through a social justice curriculum. Accessed 23 July 2020, from https://commons.clarku.edu/idce_masters_papers/25

Equalities and Human Rights Commission (2019) *Experiences. Tackling Racial Harassment: Universities Challenged*. Accessed 23 July 2020, from www.equalityhumanrights.com/sites/default/files/tackling-racial-harassment-universities-challenged.pdf

European Union Agency for Fundamental Rights and Council of Europe (2010) *Handbook on European Non-Discriminatory Law*, Brussels, Belgium: EU Publications.

Hill, J., Philpot, R., Walton-Fisette, J. L., Sutherland, S., Flemons, M., Ovens, A., Phillips, S. & Flory, S.B., (2018) Conceptualising social justice and sociocultural issues within physical education teacher education: international perspectives. *Physical Education and Sport Pedagogy*, 23(5) 469–83.

Husbands, C. & Pearce, J. (2012) *What Makes Great Pedagogy? Nine Claims from Research*, Nottingham: National College of School Leadership.

Jabbar, A. & Mirza, M. (2019) Managing diversity: academic's perspective on culture and teaching. *Race Ethnicity and Education*, 22(5), 569–88.

Jeyasingham, D. & Morton, J. (2019) How is 'racism' understood in literature about black and minority ethnic social work students in Britain? A conceptual review. *Social Work Education*, 38(5), 563–75.

Jivraj, S. (2020) Decolonizing the academy – between a rock and a hard place. *Interventions*, 22(4), 552–73.

Kishimoto, K. (2018) Anti-racist pedagogy: from faculty's self-reflection to organizing within and beyond the classroom. *Race Ethnicity and Education*, 21(4), 540–54.

Leonardo, Z. (2013) The story of schooling: critical race theory and the educational racial contract. *Discourse: Studies in the Cultural Politics of Education*, 34(4), 599–610.

Montgomery, K. (2013) Pedagogy and privilege: the challenges and possibilities of teaching critically about racism. *Critical Education*, 4(1), 1–22.

National Education Union (2019) *Framework for Developing an Anti-Racist Approach*, London: National Education Union. Accessed 23 July 2020, from https://neu.org.uk/media/11236/view

Schucan Bird, K. & Pitman, L. (2020) How diverse is your reading list? Exploring issues of representation and decolonisation in the UK. *Higher Education*, 79(2), 903–20.

Showunmi, V., Atewologun, D. & Bebbington D. (2016) Ethnic, gender and class intersections in British women's leadership experiences, *Educational Management Administration & Leadership*, 44(6), 917–35.

Singh, S. (2019) What we know about the experiences and outcomes of anti-racist social work education? An empirical case study evidencing contested and transformative learning. *Social Work Education*, 38(5), 631–53.

SOAS (2018) *Decolonising SOAS Learning and Teaching Toolkit for Programme and Module Convenors*, London: SOAS.

Tate, S. A. & Bagguley, P. (2017) Building the anti-racist university: next steps. *Race Ethnicity and Education*, 20(3), 289–99.

Wagner, A. E. (2005) Unsettling the academy: working through the challenges of anti-racist pedagogy. *Race Ethnicity and Education*, 8(3), 261–75.

13

Curriculum design

Parise Carmichael-Murphy and Eileen Ggbagbo

Introduction

Curricula are critical to student and staff learning, retention and success (Naylor & Mifsud, 2020). The notion of planning, designing and delivering curricula is imperative to HE pedagogy. Increasing conversations and discourses are concerned with decolonising the curriculum and abolishing archaic curricula designs to challenge racism in both the overt and covert curriculum.

In a report by David Batty (2020) in *The Guardian* newspaper, only 24 out of 128 universities responding to freedom of information (FoI) requests declared a commitment to decolonising the curriculum; and another 84 universities declared a commitment to making their curriculum more diverse, international or inclusive. Despite this, many current efforts to decolonise curricula are targeted specifically to limited disciplines such as History, Art, Drama or English. Of the 24 universities committed to decolonising curricula, just nine have put this in writing, with only two including it in their core strategic plan (Batty, 2020).

To decolonise the curriculum is to critique Eurocentric perspectives that dominate the UK HE and to question how, or which, aspects of curricula (re)produce inequalities. It is not an effort to exclude knowledges or remove British history, but to provide a formal space that openly interrogates the ways that

Eurocentric knowledge is positioned in academia (for example, Saini & Begum, 2020). It calls for the inclusion of diverse knowledges, diverse studies and diverse scholars to resist the longstanding omission of worldwide perspectives (for example, Gabriel, 2019). It calls for transparency and for universities to acknowledge the contemporary knowledge positioning is rooted in, and reflective of, colonial legacies (for example, Gyamera & Burke, 2018).

To date, we have seen increasing conversations around decolonising the curriculum across the whole education sector, with HE students proactively requesting for this cause over the last five years (Arshad et al, 2021). Student calls to decolonise curricula have led much of the change we have seen across universities to date. In 2015, the Rhodes Must Fall[1] movement started a conversation at the University of Oxford that sought to raise awareness of the colonial legacy of the Cecil Rhodes statue at Oxford. It further encouraged conversations around curriculum representation and discriminatory practices that saw Black, Asian and minority ethnic students under-represented. Also in 2015, Why is my Curriculum so White?[2] was founded at the University College London, where universities were dencouraged to engage in conversations around representation across reading lists and course content.

In May 2018, the Decolonising SOAS Working Group[3] provided a Learning and Teaching Toolkit for Programme and Module Conveners,[4] which offered suggestions and ideas for decolonised curriculum design. In June 2018, Keele University launched their Manifesto for Decolonising the Curriculum,[5] which built upon conversations led by the Why is my Curriculum so White? movement. In early 2020, De Montfort University launched Decolonising DMU,[6] which promotes co-production of the curriculum with students to ensure that they are truly diversified in design, production and content. As of May 2020, the Black Lives Matter (BLM)[7] movement has garnered unprecedented public support in the UK and this has led to further calls for British curricula to accurately reflect the achievements and contributions of Black people, while more honestly reflecting the process by which knowledge is valued in Britain today.

Anne Kimunguyi describes a colonial curriculum as 'unrepresentative, inaccessible, and privileged' (Staff Development Forum, 2020). The Black Asian and Minority Ethnic awarding gap identified that there is a 13 per cent gap between the likelihood of White students and students from Black, Asian and minority ethnic backgrounds achieving a First or a 2:1 degree (Universities UK and National Union of Students, 2019), which could suggest that contemporary learning is inaccessible to certain groups of students. In 2017, Birmingham City University introduced the first UK undergraduate degree in Black Studies,[8] which centres on the experience, perspectives and contributions of people of the African diaspora and Kehinde Andrews (2016) argues that this will change both the face and nature of university education. As well as the development of Black Studies, we see the introduction of Critical Race Theory and Postcolonial Studies emerging as a result of student and scholarly demand (Pimblott, 2020).

Voice of the authors

Co-author

'I am not free while any woman is unfree, even when her shackles are very different from my own' (Lorde, 1984). It is not uncommon that I battle to assimilate my own perspective and thought with what I have been and continue to be told within formal education. Only recently have I found confidence as a PhD researcher in Education to look beyond the ivory tower, to truly begin to understand myself and the thoughts that I generate. I engage with bodies of Black feminist thought, which confirm to me that my epistemology is not invalid, under-researched, or uncertain – but that it has been and continues to be devalued, silenced and marginalised.

I was fortunate that my undergraduate degree in Early Childhood Studies encouraged me to champion empowering and emancipatory education, but I also recognise that these ideas hold limited value among a political climate of individualisation. The discourse of social mobility and meritocracy that filters through HE equality and diversity rhetoric has not left me feeling included, but astutely aware of the aspects of my identity that I must mute or leave behind to feel 'included' in UK HE.

I draw upon Lorde's (1984) *Sister Outsider* regularly, as it helps me understand how to balance myself precariously both inside and outside academic communities. I draw much confidence from Lorde's collection of essays and speeches, and I take pride in promoting diverse knowledges that are produced within HE but also recognise the cultural richness of knowledges that can be found outside. I now look for the practices that sustain inequalities and I recognise how knowledges that align with my epistemological stance have been excluded from the curriculum across all stages of education, and the impact and influence this has on my precarious positioning within my community, academic community and the UK.

Yet, I'm left to question what other diverse knowledges have been devalued and I wonder just how decolonised my own mind really is. So, while I sit on the academic periphery, I encourage you to question just how free your thoughts are inside the ivory tower when they are generated within a space that confines others' thoughts so strictly. Audre Lorde reminds us that diverse knowledges should be praised for enriching, not threatening, our lives. Each day, I still ask myself who specifically is threatened by diverse knowledges and, more specifically, what exactly is it that they want to preserve?

Co-author

In a Politics seminar, a lecturer asked what we knew about Hitler's economic policies. He specifically called on my friend, who replied that she did not know. He then mocked her in front of the rest of the class and insinuated that she could not possibly be interested in studying Politics if she did not know this detail about Hitler's Germany. As an international student from Nigeria, she explained that being educated in the Global South meant that she did not have extensive knowledge of Germany during the interwar period. But she can talk about the impact of the economic policies of Ibrahim Babagida – a Nigerian military dictator.

This incident highlights the need for flexibility in curriculum design that allows for more local case studies in order for students to gain an intimate understanding of various concepts.

In academia, ideas, concepts and theories do not exist in a vacuum and are made stronger when they can be applied to a variety of case studies internationally and across time. Similarly, in pedagogy, students do not retain knowledge in an arbitrary vacuum. And so, studying is more effective when it can be applied to the world around them. This allows diversity into curriculum design that has various positive impacts, such as the development of critical thinking skills.

Teaching students the skill of critical thinking requires the flexibility of using local case studies and examples. In teaching and explaining a concept in HE, students should not readily accept assumptions. They must be able to challenge these assumptions and apply them to various scenarios to ensure that they hold weight in dialogue. By using localised case studies, not only do individual students retain information and deepen their critical understanding, but all students can participate in a richer dialogue that enables more critical arguments to be produced.

In the experience that I shared previously, shifting the focus away from one case study in the West, and allowing multiple case studies from various regions and time periods would have helped us as students to fully grasp the variety of economic ideologies and the multiplicity in their implications. Personally, my baseline assumptions would have been more accurate, which would have been reflected in the essays I produced for that module, as well as others.

Therefore, in allowing the flexibility of using localised case studies in curriculum design, students internalise that there are multiple ways of seeing the world, which have unique advantages when it comes to theorising on the causes and impacts of events and ideologies. In addition, it is a crucial first step in leaving room for decolonial pedagogies and tackling racist blind spots in the curriculum design.

Change domains

Acknowledging colonial legacies

To truly decolonise the curriculum, universities must acknowledge the colonial legacies of the institution and how they shape experiences for students and staff today. The National

Union of Students (2019) released a Plan for Action manifesto for 2019–2020,[9] which describes educational structures and institutions as a 'product of colonialism' and identifies that some have profited directly from this, while others have perpetuated 'systems that assure White privilege' and contribute to the racial inequities prevalent among UK HE today. Although sparse, some UK HE commitment to colonial transparency has been identified.

In 2009, UCL generated the Legacies of British Slavery[10] database, which illustrates how modern Britain's economy, politics and culture was shaped by slavery, including the compensation given to the Government when slavery was abolished. In April 2019, the University of Cambridge announced a two-year enquiry into how it benefited from the slave trade and to what extent scholarship at the university reinforced racialised differences.[11] Most recently, in August 2019, the University of Glasgow agreed to pay reparations after acknowledging that they benefited financially from the slave trade, and their Slavery, Abolition and the University of Glasgow[12] report is the first to address this in the UK.

Addressing the reproduction of power hierarchies

Decolonising teaching and learning should go beyond just the acknowledgement of colonial legacies to challenge and change the current structures that marginalise students and staff. The Universities UK Black, Asian and minority ethnic attainment gap report argued that universities need a culture change, one which clearly acknowledges that issues of race are embedded within wider strategic goals. At present, White upper-class heterosexual cisgender men intersectionally experience greater privilege than minoritised groups, which is rooted in the colonial and capitalist history of Britain as we know it today (Mngomezulu & Hadebe, 2018). A decolonised curriculum empowers university staff and students; it recognises the hegemonic and Eurocentric pedagogy that has distorted contemporary knowledge value in UK HE, openly acknowledging the past and present role of the university in the (re)production of colonial legacies and unequal power distribution. Universities must acknowledge that defining the curriculum for others is an act of power and must take ethical responsibility in acknowledging that the reproduction of traditional knowledges is rooted in power.

Embracing diverse knowledges

The decolonising movements require HE to embrace alternative knowledges, tools and scholars that inform diverse disciplines and approaches to teaching and learning. A report from the Open University, Innovating Pedagogy (Ferguson et al, 2019), describes a curriculum as 'a way of identifying the knowledge we value' and providing structure to how we are 'taught to think and talk about the world'. Universities should embrace the multiplicity of teaching and learning and actively recognise how it can be more easily accessible or inaccessible for racialised and/or minoritised groups in society. Efforts to recognise and credit Black scholars are evidenced in HE responses to the 2020 BLM movements, but these efforts must not be just tokenistic inclusion. The 'inclusion' of Black, Asian and minority ethnic authors on reading and reference lists alone does not encourage us to think critically about how or why they were not included in the first place.

Implementing anti-racist pedagogy

EDI rhetoric often leads to a tokenistic approach such as the promoted *inclusion* of non-White scholars on singular subject reading lists (for example, Science, History, English Literature; Bird & Pitman, 2020). However, the decolonisation of curricula should take a holistic approach and be reflected throughout the HE sector. It should reach beyond just drawing upon diverse scholars to broaden contemporary perspectives, and revisit what has dominated the curriculum thus far, with a critical lens to identity privileges and ultimately address social inequalities. Further, not only does critical education benefit the individual development of those who participate in learning and/or teaching, but it also offers great potential to transform beyond the personal level via subject disciplines, the university and society.

Actively listening to student voices

To date, universities' formal commitments to decolonising their curricula have been limited, but instead, we acknowledge the contemporary movements by stakeholders that demand that the curriculum is decolonised and diversified. The majority of calls to decolonise the curriculum originate from the 2015 Rhodes Must Fall movement in Cape Town, South Africa; since then, students across the UK have mobilised against the iconography at universities that promote colonial wealth and power imbalances. Student-led movements demand that universities seek to 'decolonise the curriculum'; most notably, students and their unions have led, supported and engaged in movements such as Rhodes Must Fall (2015) at the University of Oxford, and Why is my Curriculum so White? (2015) at University College London. Subsequently, students should be involved in the co-production of curricula, and student unions, societies and other groups should be supported as bodies who represent diverse student groups more appropriately.

Enabling global citizenship

As university education is globalised, the assumptions that underpin the Eurocentric 'knowledge society' that dominates HE teaching and learning have been challenged by communities (Universities UK and National Union of Students, 2019). University curricula should strive to enable students to develop as global citizens; otherwise, there is a danger of (re)producing colonial practices. Clifford & Montgomery (2014) describe global citizens as:

1. Having a critical knowledge of their self, culture and social-historical positioning.
2. Having knowledge of other cultures and peoples.
3. Having recognition of the interdependence of all humans.
4. Having knowledge of global issues and moral sensitivity to social injustice, inequality and racism.

5. Actively pursuing a life that does not benefit themselves to the disadvantage of others.

These are critical provocations that can enable a more globally inclusive curriculum and be embedded in undoing colonial adversities that exist in curricula.

Allowing localised case studies and experiential examples

The purpose of HE is to equip students to understand the world and to work towards transforming society to be more just and equitable. That begins by allowing students to critically assess and understand their immediate environments. Localised case studies and experiential examples speak to a decolonial pedagogy, as they remove the hierarchical nature of learning in a classroom that favours students from more privileged backgrounds that have had prior access to theories and ideas from the West. They also pluralise the subjects of enquiry, which is contrary to the dominant approach in Western scholarship, thus giving equal value to all forms of knowledge.

Black and postcolonial feminist literature engages difference as a means of humanising students and their learning process. They often centre autobiographical ways of knowing in order to make epistemological interventions that challenge the explicit Whiteness, Eurocentrism and norms of knowledge production within mainstream curriculum design. As a blueprint, allowing localised case studies as well as experiential examples as part of a curriculum enables a more intimate understanding of the world and develops the critical thinking skills of students.

Centring decolonial content in core introductory modules

Through lived experiences as an International Relations student, the courses that had the most content surrounding empire or that explicitly acknowledged race have been specialist modules that I could only access in my final year. However, I found the content and reading lists to be introductory and the facilitation of discussions to be surface level. HE institutions often respond to demands to decolonise the curriculum by including one lecture about race, or adding a Black scholar to the reading list, or hiring one staff member to teach a specialist course on race that is capped. This reinforces the hierarchy of Western scholarship over other, often more critical, scholarship that addresses racism and the legacies of colonialism.

In designing a curriculum that seeks to address and challenge racism, decolonial concepts and literature must form the centre of introductory courses. This is because they are often mandatory for all students and will therefore aid in the formation of their critical thinking. This would also remove the onus on students of colour that are often called upon to generate conversations around decolonisation or highlight racist arguments or thinking that ultimately hinders their retention in these classes.

Assessment diversification and innovation

Traditional forms of assessment such as end-of-teaching, sit-down exams do not accurately reflect a student's engagement with the course content. Furthermore, with the national Black, Asian and minority ethnic attainment gap being 13 per cent, as of May 2019, it is clear that traditional HE assessment structures disadvantage students of colour.

When implementing localised case studies and experiential examples into teaching and discussions, it must also be followed by an assessment structure that reflects this form of teaching. For example, rather than a set list of predetermined questions for coursework examinations, students should be given the opportunity to develop questions based on empirical puzzles that are informed by their interests and experiences.

In addition to that, encouraging the use of literature beyond the reading list should not be limited to formal academic scholarship, but should recognise poetry, music, film and everyday anecdotes as valuable contributions and interventions. In this way, gauging students' (and even staff) engagement with the course material and their level of critical thinking is more accurate and removes the inaccessibility of refined academic words (big words) that leads to the imposter syndrome barrier that students of colour often speak of when it comes to assessments.

Developing innovation in teaching

In HE, the purpose of the academic is to facilitate discussions to deepen the knowledge around concepts, ideas and theories. Often, however, teachers tend to be more instructional – anticipating the needs of the class as a collective rather than taking a more flexible approach such as presenting a problem that links to the topic of discussion and encouraging dialogue that unpacks the situation and moves towards potential solutions. This moves away from traditional teaching methods that do not have high retention rates for students.

Furthermore, traditional teaching methods are often based on implicit racist biases that assume a privileged and White baseline level of knowledge as universal. Yet, in allowing for more experiential ways of knowing, a comfortable, anti-racist and non-hierarchical academic environment is created in which all members of the class feel valued as equals and can actively participate in discussions and debates. Creativity in teaching, assessment and content design does not treat students as a monolith but enables students to develop their critical voices and analytic skills.

This is by no means an exhaustive list of areas for critical decolonial and anti-racist change within the curriculum design of universities. However, this list should form the basis of an ongoing imperative to critically assess areas of racism implicit and explicit within the HE curriculum design. These areas should not be considered in isolation but should be complimentary in implementation in order to achieve the best results.

Reflective questions

- How do colonial legacies privilege students' attainment and experience of teaching and learning differently?[13]
- How does the university take responsibility for enabling open and transparent conversations about colonial legacies?[14]
- In viewing students as a monolith neoliberal consumer of HE, how can they be equipped to understand the plurality of the world?[15]

- How can you enable students and/or colleagues to be empowered and challenge racist discourse, pedagogy and practice?[16]
- How do you promote diverse knowledges in your teaching and/or research practice?[17]
- How can you address the exclusionary nature of introductory courses and modules?[18]
- How do administrative practices or processes restrict or enable student and staff experiences and access to support?[19]
- How can you contribute to the holistic anti-racist learning and development of students?[20]
- What can you do both inside *and* outside the university to empower yourself and others?[21]
- What assumptions have you already made about your course and how can these be racist and exclusionary?
- What forms of learning and ways of knowing do you value?
- How limited is your understanding of what constitutes academic scholarship and how could that be racist and exclusionary?

Notes

[1]   https://rmfoxford.wordpress.com/
[2]   https://www.nusconnect.org.uk/articles/why-is-my-curriculum-White-decolonising-the-academy#:~:text=%E2%80%98Why%20is%20My%20Curriculum%20White%3F%E2%80%99%20is%20a%20question,Birmingham%2C%20and%20Manchester%2C%20and%20an%20unwavering%20online%20presence
[3]   https://blogs.soas.ac.uk/decolonisingsoas/
[4]   https://blogs.soas.ac.uk/decolonisingsoas/learning-teaching/toolkit-for-programme-and-module-convenors/
[5]   https://www.keele.ac.uk/equalitydiversity/equalityframeworksandactivities/equalityawardsandreports/equalityawards/raceequalitycharter/keeledecolonisingthecurriculumnetwork/#keele-manifesto-for-decolonising-the-curriculum
[6]   https://decolonisingdmu.our.dmu.ac.uk/
[7]   https://www.blacklivesmatter.uk/
[8]   https://www.bcu.ac.uk/social-sciences/research/identities-and-inequalities/research-clusters/black-studies
[9]   https://www.nusconnect.org.uk/resources/nus-uk-plan-for-action
[10] https://www.ucl.ac.uk/lbs/
[11] https://www.thetimes.co.uk/article/cambridge-university-to-examine-its-links-to-slave-trade-0lpvk5vkb

12 https://www.gla.ac.uk/media/Media_607547_smxx.pdf

13 An intersectional approach to explore student attainment is needed, one which considers how social identity markers such as race, gender, class and ability impact students' inclusion/exclusion at the university collectively. Education policy tends to adopt a 'one-size-fits-all' approach, which fails to think about within-group differences that impact student attainment differently. Beyond thinking about Black, Asian and minority ethnic attainment, university teaching and learning needs to reflect the diverse populations that come under the umbrella term to avoid the further exclusion of minoritised and/or racialised groups.

14 Staff and students should be empowered to engage in dialogue that embraces diverse knowledges to inform the strategic planning of teaching and learning; this requires access to spaces and resources that reflect diverse cultures. If the university commits to decolonising, it is imperative that there is acknowledgement of what 'to decolonise' really means. Open and transparent communications are needed to empower staff and students, enabling them to honestly reflect on the historical legacies that inform UK HE curricula today.

15 Students are the prime consumers of HE, yet HE policies and curriculum design do not cater to the pluralities in identities of these students. Inclusive education policies are in place to tackle this, but how different would the educational experience of students of colour be if the diversity of their realities were reflected in fundamental policies instead of as an additional policy? Rather than being 'included', anti-racist and equality policies should actively form the basis of all student engagement policies.

16 Teaching and research staff should acknowledge the power given to their position within the university and take some responsibility for contributing individually to spaces in which students and/or colleagues are enabled to engage in discussions that respectfully challenge past and present knowledge and practice.

17 Academic staff need to take an active role in critical and reflective practice. To ensure that teaching, learning and research are accessible for diverse groups of students, staff should reflect on what information they include, why they are including it and how they are presenting it – who exactly is this knowledge for and is this explicit?

18 Introductory modules often rely on a baseline assumption of knowledge that favours students from privileged backgrounds. Black, Asian and minority ethnic students then face a mountain in order to catch up with their White peers in feeling confident enough in their knowledge, skills and lived experience to participate in discussions. This defeats the purpose of an introductory module and establishes a hierarchy of knowledge that sustains the Black, Asian and minority ethnic attainment gap.

19 Professional staff should reflect on whether there are clear procedures for staff and/or students to give feedback on university curricula, and where not, how they could make these clearer and more explicit.

20 Learning does not only take place in the classroom, but also in the interactions outside of the classroom. In acknowledging that racism is pervasive in all aspects of society, what forms of non-academic learning equip students to directly challenge racism?

21 Although many of us attend university to acquire specific knowledge(s) to achieve the specific end goal of employment, students should not rely on the university to provide knowledge that empowers as individuals. Diverse knowledges are generated outside the university, and we should make it one of our aims as learners to bring these inside. Connect with the Student Union, join a society, volunteer at a charity, attend community centres and groups, talk with your family and friends – and take pride in the diverse knowledges generated within these places.

References

Andrews, K. (2016) At last, the UK has a black studies university course. It's long overdue. *The Guardian*. Accessed 9 February 2022, from www.theguardian.com/commentisfree/2016/may/20/black-studies-university-course-long-overdue

Arshad, M., Dada, R. S., Elliott, C., Kalinowska, I., Khan, M., Lipinski, R. J., Vassanth, V., Bhandal, J., de Quinto Schneider, M., Georgis, I. & Shilston, F. (2021) Diversity or decolonization? Searching for the tools to dismantle the 'master's house'. *London Review of Education*, 19(1), 1–18. DOI: 10.14324/lre.19.1.19.

Batty, D. (2020) Only a fifth of UK universities say they are 'decolonising' curriculum. *The Guardian*. Accessed 9 February 2022, from www.theguardian.com/us-news/2020/jun/11/only-fifth-of-uk-universities-have-said-they-will-decolonise-curriculum

Bird, K. S. & Pitman, L. (2020) How diverse is your reading list? Exploring issues of representation and decolonisation in the UK. *Higher Education*, 79(5), 903–20.

Clifford, V. & Montgomery, C. (2014) Challenging conceptions of western higher education and promoting graduates as global citizens. *Higher Education Quarterly*, 68(1), 28–45. DOI: 10.1111/hequ.12029.

Decolonising SOAS Working Group (2018) *Decolonising SOAS Learning and Teaching Toolkit for Programme and Module Convenors*, London: SOAS University of London. Accessed 9 February 2022, from https://blogs.soas.ac.uk/decolonisingsoas/learning-teaching/

Ferguson, R., Coughlan, T., Egelandsdal, K., Gaved, M., Herodotou, C., Hillaire, G., Jones, D., Jowers, I., Kukulska-Hulme, A., McAndrew, P., Misiejuk, K., Ness, I. J., Rienties, B., Scanlon, E., Sharples, M., Wasson, B., Weller, M. & Whitelock, D. (2019) Innovating Pedagogy 2019: Open University Innovation Report 7. Accessed 9 February 2022, from https://iet.open.ac.uk/file/innovating-pedagogy-2019.pdf

Gabriel, D. (2019) Enhancing higher education practice through the 3D pedagogy framework to decolonize, democratize and diversify the curriculum. *International Journal of Technology and Inclusive Education*, 8(2), 1459–66.

Gyamera, G. O. & Burke, P. J. (2018) Neoliberalism and curriculum in higher education: a post-colonial analyses. *Teaching in Higher Education*, 23(4), 450–67.

Lorde, A. (1984) *Sister Outsider: Essays and Speeches by Audre Lorde*. California: Crossing Press.

Mngomezulu, B. R. & Hadebe, S. (2018) What would the decolonisation of a political science curriculum entail? Lessons to be learnt from the East African experience at the Federal University of East Africa. *Politikon*, 45(1), 66–80. DOI: 10.1080/02589346.2018.1418205.

Naylor, R. & Mifsud, N. (2020) Towards a structural inequality framework for student retention and success. *Higher Education Research & Development*, 39(2), 259–72.

Pimblott, K. (2020) Decolonising the university: the origins and meaning of a movement. *The Political Quarterly*, 91(1), 210–16. DOI: 10.1111/1467-923X.12784.

Saini, R. & Begum, N. (2020) Demarcation and definition: explicating the meaning and scope of 'decolonisation' in the social and political sciences. *The Political Quarterly*, 91(1), 217–21.

Staff Development Forum (2020) Decolonisation of the curriculum: a conversation. Accessed 9 February 2022, from https://sdf.ac.uk/6985/decolonisation-of-the-curriculum-a-conversation

Universities UK and National Union of Students (2019) Black, Asian and minority ethnic student attainment at UK universities. Accessed 9 February 2022, from www.universitiesuk.ac.uk/sites/default/files/field/downloads/2021-07/bame-student-attainment.pdf

14

University identity

Briana Coles and Arun Verma

Introduction

Brands, marketing and communications across universities have become increasingly competitive to engage national and international audiences to come to study at a UK university (Bamberger, Bronshtein & Yemini, 2020). UK universities are under pressure to continuously have a clear brand narrative and corporate visual identities, with a view to striving to be agile, modernised, global and relevant (Mogaji, 2018). However, the identities of some universities are masked behind racist and colonial histories (Gabriel & Tate, 2017). This chapter provides an outline for how universities can meaningfully disrupt their brand to start becoming anti-racist. Universities typically develop their brand around their location, courses, student experience, credibility and career outcomes (Mogaji & Yoon, 2019), but neglect equity and EDI as part of the brand, marketing and communication guiding principles.

Universities' identities are intrinsically connected to the White structures of colonialism (Doku, 2019) and radicalisation (Law, 2016). It is not possible to dismantle structural racism in a university without recognising its links to White privilege and its impact on the oppression of Black, Asian and minority ethnic people in the UK university system. Law (2016) outlines several issues that disarm universities from addressing their colonial and saviourism brands and identities and these concern the following areas: failing to hold leadership accountable and restoring anti-racism as a foundational intellectual project; narrowing the debate concerning race and HE; deprioritising the anti-racist good practice model in institutional identities; marginalising debates about race in HE; and overlooking cross-sectoral and cross-national learning. Disinvestment from addressing these in an HE institution's brand narrative, identity, communication and marketing can exacerbate the dearth of diversity and inclusion in university spaces.

Some of these themes are conveyed in universities' professional services where 'the use of images of racialised staff in university promotional material also attracted comment. Institutions could use them as positive messages that show the institution is not a 'White' enclave. Conversely, using such images could be viewed as tokenistic or perfunctory when the images do not match the real university environment. Mirza (2017) repeatedly requested that her photo be removed from college brochures, arguing that '[v]isual images of "colourful" happy faces are used to show how the university has embraced the difference' (Mahony & Weiner, 2020, p 850). This is not to argue against the use of diversity in imagery; however, such imagery is needed to mirror the diversity of the university population and their strategic priorities. This alignment is critical to moving past performativity and cultivating brand, marketing and communication opportunities that are substantiated by a real anti-racist movement.

Lacking a voice

There is limited research exploring the diverse voices in HE functions concerning brands, marketing and communication. The existing research mostly focuses on exploring the ways in which universities cultivate and nurture their brand identities, along with the kinds of messaging the universities endeavour to communicate (for example, Chapleo, Carrillo Durán & Castillo Díaz, 2011; Mogaji & Yoon, 2019; Sobande, 2020). The literature does not examine the HE brand, marketing and communication functions through race equality and intersectionality. Understanding the ways in which Black, Asian and minority ethnic communities perceive how universities, brand, market and communicate themselves locally and globally can provide a unique insight into widening access, participation and reaching diverse communities and talent for the HE sector. It would also be important to speak with those working in HE brand, communication and marketing functions to investigate the role of anti-racism, equality and wider diversity themes in these functions.

Change domains

Enhancing the co-design and co-creation of brand and communication strategies

HE institutions must consider how they meaningfully engage Black, Asian and minority ethnic staff, students and local communities in developing and steering the design and delivery of brand, marketing and communication campaigns. Participatory design and action can ensure that marketing and communication functions consider the formal, informal, direct and indirect impacts of the communications. Diversity in these functions enables a critical and thoughtful lens through which the content and mode of delivery to staff and students are culturally sensitive and considered, particularly during wider events, for example, BLM.

The role of intersectionality

Brand, marketing and communication functions within HE institutions play a powerful role for both the university and local community in fully understanding and demystifying language associated with race equality, decolonisation and anti-racism, particularly during a time when there is misinterpretation of anti-racist language. HE institutions must embody the core values of anti-racism premised in celebrating diversity and advancing inclusion. Such functions play a crucial role in universities' internationalisation and global agendas, and the HE marketing and communications team could be leading the sector to ensure that global and international communication teams are provided with the knowledge and confidence to apply both intersectional and decolonial approaches to global partnerships and working. This example could position UK universities as international leaders in this area.

Imagery and visuals

HE institutions need to critically consider the ways in which they use images and symbolism in their internal and external communications. Universities must avoid White gaze, White saviourism and tokenistic approaches to developing communications and marketing products and items for circulation. As with issues of volunteer tourism (for example, Cowden, 2020), it is important for HE institutions to ensure that images of Black, Asian and minority ethnic people are not thrown into brochures to fill quotas, raise the profile of the university or react to wider external events. Black, Asian and minority ethnic people who are included in university marketing materials must provide consent and must be included in steering the visual story. Such imagery needs to be substantiated by race equity being considered as a priority for the HE institution and enable racialised and minoritised communities to meaningfully participate in decision making and transformation.

Reflective questions

- How many of your brand, communication and marketing staff are confident in anti-racism?
- Is racial inequality and White gaze present in your brand, communication and marketing strategies and implementation plans within your institution?
- Do racial inequalities and Whitewashing of communications affect staff or students more?
- Does authentic representation in marketing, communications and branding matter to you?
- What effect do you think it has on Black, Asian and minority ethnic students when you are not actively diversifying your communications, marketing and branding?
- What actions have you taken to address anti-racism in your marketing and communications strategic plan?

- Is senior leadership doing enough to improve diversity and inclusion in the function of your department?
- Is diversity treated as a critical component of your institution's communication, branding and marketing ethos?
- Is the degree of racial inequality in your approach to communicating with students more or less than that of society at large?
- What are you, personally, doing to amplify the voices of people of colour?
- Is it a Black, Asian and minority ethnic student or staff member's role to continuously explain racism to you when you are sending a communication note to all staff and students?
- Do you shy away from conversations about Black lives, racism and ethnic discrimination when thinking about your marketing and communications approach?
- Do you critically question the communications and marketing resources and materials that you receive with a racial equality lens?
- Is being anti-racist an active or passive pursuit when communicating work internally and externally?
- Is what you are reposting on social media channels harmful to Black, Asian and/or minority ethnic peers in your university?

References

Bamberger, A., Bronshtein, Y. & Yemini, M. (2020) Marketing universities and targeting international students: a comparative analysis of social media data trails. *Teaching in Higher Education*, 25(4), 476–92.

Chapleo, C., Carrillo Durán, M. V. & Castillo Díaz, A. (2011) Do UK universities communicate their brands effectively through their websites?. *Journal of Marketing for Higher Education*, 21(1), 25–46. DOI:10.1080/08841241.2011.569589.

Cowden, J. (2020) New colonialists of Africa? Tackling the white saviour complex in contemporary voluntourism. *Critical Reflections: A Student Journal on Contemporary Sociological Issues*. Accessed 1 February 2021, from https://160.9.152.173/index. php/SOC/article/view/4603.

Doku, A. (2019) Recognising British colonialism and advancing the Academy. Advance HE. Accessed 1 February 2021, from www.advance-he.ac.uk/news-and-views/Recognising-British-colonialism-and-advancing-the-Academy

Gabriel, D. & Tate, S. A. (2017) *Inside the Ivory Tower: Narratives of Women of Colour Surviving and Thriving in British Academia.* London: Trentham Books.

Law, I. (2016) Building the anti-racist university, action and new agendas. *Race Ethnicity and Education,* 20(3), 332–43. DOI: 10.1080/13613324.2016.1260232.

Mahony, P. & Weiner, G. (2020) 'Getting in, getting on, getting out': Black, Asian and minority ethnic staff in UK higher education. *Race Ethnicity and Education,* 1–17.

Mirza, H. S. (2017) 'One in a million': a journey of a post-colonial woman of colour in the white academy. In D. Gabriel and S. A. Tate (eds), *Inside the Ivory Tower: Narratives of Women of Colour Surviving and Thriving in British Academia.* London: Trentham Books.

Mogaji, E. (2018) UK universities' corporate visual identities (version 1). DOI: 10.31124/advance.7203269.v1.

Mogaji, E. & Yoon, H. (2019) Thematic analysis of marketing messages in UK universities' prospectuses. *International Journal of Educational Management,* 33(7) 1561–81. DOI: 10.1108/IJEM-05-2018-0149.

Sobande, F. (2020) Woke-washing: 'intersectional' femvertising and branding 'woke' bravery. *European Journal of Marketing,* 54(11) 2723–45. DOI: 10.1108/EJM-02-2019-0134.

15

Educational professionalism

Deya Mukherjee

Introduction

Professionalism as a concept requires staff and students to behave with integrity during the university experience (Van der Sluis, Burden & Huet, 2017). This theme directly tackles what anti-racist professionalism could be and look like for a university. 'Professionalism' is a code (Sethy, 2018). This is true both in its role as a code of conduct, written and unwritten rules for behaviour within a workplace, and as a system of meaning that is designed to include a select group of people while maintaining the illusion of inclusion for all. It is no coincidence, for example, that the concept is associated with roles and industries that have often been gatekept from working-class communities.

Scrutinising the notion of professionalism and its respective responsibilities and attributes further, from within a culture where the concept of 'work' and the places we do it in have been moulded by racial capitalism (Mehri, 2020), reveals them as mechanisms of maintaining an exploitative status quo. Dominant themes covered in critiques of the concept of 'professionalism' concern the double standards of behaviour for marginalised staff that relate to oppressive stereotypes within being and acting professionally (Rios, 2015). Codes of 'civility' and 'politeness' flatten the historic roots and inherently traumatic nature of experiencing oppression, and demand a lack of emotion on the part of the marginalised when encountering racism, while allowing for racist and anti-Black behaviour that is presented through the lens of 'politeness' (Pillay, 2015).

When exploring the wider systemic influences, we see the ways in which capitalism-engendered means of subjugation, such as gentrification, shape the ways racialised communities, and Black communities in particular, are policed by the concept (Uddin, 2020).

The ways in which the concept of professionalism is used to enforce a 'you're not welcome here' message through every individual aspect of being, for example, clothing, language, hair and food, require marginalised employees, and Black employees, to 'shrink themselves' to assimilate (Gray, 2019).

It is no coincidence that the 'professional' as a racialised concept is reminiscent of racialised concepts of 'tidiness' and 'propriety' as levied in uniform policies against school children from racialised communities (Dabiri, 2020), with numerous cases of Black children being excluded from UK schools because their natural hair was deemed as 'not meeting school uniform requirements' (Joseph-Salisbury, 2020). These codes of presentation are linked because barring Black, Asian and minority ethnic communities, and Black communities in particular, from schooling in this way directly influences who is permitted entrance into the 'professional' workplace.

Common routes to employment within a university context, along with not acknowledging systemic classism and racism when identifying skills or educational 'gaps' in prospective employees, tend to frame the employment trajectories accessible to White, middle-class workers as the only valid pathways of experience. Further to this, universities tend to employ systems that completely negate the possibility that racism might be a commonplace experience for global majority workers (as noted in Brookfield, 2014). For example, application forms often have mandatory 'reason for leaving' boxes. These boxes force applicants who may be trying to leave a racist work environment to put an emotionally damaging 'positive spin' on the situation for the sake of employment. Similarly, forms often stress the necessity of references needing to be from the applicant's current line manager. Given the prevalence of racist behaviour from line managers, reassurance could be given that individual circumstances will be considered, and alternative avenues for workplace references could be further explored (Rollock, 2019).

For those who are able to access the workplace, a culture of workplace 'loyalty' can mean being asked to consider 'reputational damage' when making a case for race equity initiatives or being tokenised by the organisation as a means to 'prove' how 'inclusive' they are (UCU, 2016). Commonly, the language used by universities making public or all staff statements addressing institutional racism is that they are not 'immune' to wider problems of systemic racism. However, rather than the passive role implied by this word, academia has often been historically critical in the formation of the racist ideologies (Saini, 2019) that have shaped our contemporary global context (Kubota, 2019), and specifically the idea that racialised people are subjects, not scholars, diminishing the professional value of Black, Asian and/or minority ethnic staff.

When thinking about the university as a workplace and teaching institution, we must therefore understand the roots of the professional and 'social contract' that its employment and pedagogical framework has been built upon (that is, Tate & Page, 2018). Within this context, simply framing racial equity as a problem of mere numbers is inadequate, as an increase of students and staff from racialised communities does not change this professional 'contract', and those staff and students will be subjected to a sanctioned hostile environment, which we see today embedded in academic teaching, learning and peer relationships, with reports from UK universities of Black, Asian and minority ethnic students (Akel, 2019) and Black, Asian and minority ethnic teachers experiencing racism and anti-Blackness in the teaching environment (Sian, 2017), from students and teachers alike. The possibility of racial harassment within professional colleague relations is not reflected within professionalism frameworks, despite being experienced widely across academic and non-academic university departments (Equality and Human Rights Commission, 2019). Similarly, discourses in educational professionalism do not consider racism within manager and employee relationships, despite common reports of Black, Asian and minority ethnic employees being 'taxed' in their roles with more labour expected than their White counterparts, experiences of overt racism and the prevalence of managers as barriers to promotion, along with the minimising of racism from other team members (UCU, 2016).

Furthermore, it is important to examine the role of HR in enforcing 'professional' behavioural standards that erase experiences and practices of racism, with reports of HR acting in the interests of the university as opposed to the employee when formal complaints of racism are lodged, fulfilling its historical role to approach employee issues through the lens of liability and 'threats' to the company. When there is a programme of work to consider professionalism, the evidence and literature presented here showcases that professionalism frameworks are perpetuating racism in educational environments and spaces, rather than dismantling them.

Voice of the author

One of the most troubling times I witnessed racist behaviour at a university was a very worrying pattern of overt racism from a White manager who was working specifically on increasing access to the university for marginalised communities. When I tried to bring this up with the person involved, I was told that the events I was recounting could not have happened. When I tried to seek support from my direct manager, the incidents were brushed off as 'not a big deal', even though I expressed concern since this manager was working directly with the community they were being racist towards.

The piece of work they were supposedly leading on, incidentally, had been developed by another junior employee of colour, but due to the contradictions inherent to employing Black, Asian and minority ethnic people to work on anti-racism initiatives in universities while having to answer to White managers who might not understand the issues at hand, the work was framed to others outside of the department as having been developed and led on by this White manager.

This really highlighted to me the prevalence of departments working on so-called institutional culture change as apologists for existing institutional cultures, and the dire need for radical, anti-racist practice that truly resists and seeks to remake the existing institutional culture.

Change domains

The efficacy of policy and process

Rather than a reactive approach to racism, take it as a given that racism exists in your systems and remake your professional code of conduct towards an explicitly anti-oppression framework. Pay people with relevant experience to go through your policies and HR systems, identify where they might interact with Black, Asian and minority ethnic communities in harmful ways, evaluate what 'professionalism' might be covering and rethink what an anti-racist code of conduct might really look like.

Examples of aspects of your behavioural code to scrutinise might include the ramifications of your current dress code for non-White workers, considering who might be silenced by 'loyalty' codes and how fit for purpose your anti-harassment and 'acceptable behaviour' policies are, given that codes of 'professionalism' can render applying the word 'racism' to the behaviour of a superior 'unprofessional'. Accompany this with proactive, easily accessible messaging, and specific training for everyone with line management responsibilities, on your change of approach.

Given that part of the traditional work of the word 'professionalism' in the White, middle-class workplace has been to prevent Black and Brown workers calling out racial harassment in their workplaces, developing effective systems to report racial harassment and access support is crucial. Employ a team specifically to work on implementing, managing and evaluating a joined-up, university-wide incident reporting system for all staff and students, both for data collection but also specifically as a means of accessing support where going through a line manager is not a possibility. Ensure that it safeguards and supports victims, and that the process is transparent and easy to use. Proactively disseminate information on the system and ensure it is easy to find and access. Reporting systems should be used to get to know the landscape of what racial harassment really looks like at your university as a means for further action, for which building trust in the system and evaluating impact are key. Make sure that data collected is properly analysed and used to inform policy and action, and improvement of reporting methods themselves. However, be aware of the limitations of quantitative data, and that building trust in reporting systems is a continual, long-haul process. Anyone who is responsible for dealing with harassment complaints should be professionally trained in anti-oppressive practices. One way to do this might be to establish the team who manages the reporting system as in dialogue with but separate from HR who can provide confidential, impartial, case-appropriate support for victims, develop a system that allows for the complexities of oppressive behaviour and work on solutions for culture change (for example, educational pathways and restorative justice processes where appropriate).

Implement well-resourced and mandatory anti-oppression training for all staff and students that breaks with the traditionally favoured 'floating brains' model of unconscious bias training that leans heavily into the idea that oppressing people is a 'natural' human tendency that is out of our control. Allocate resources to the development of training that focuses on the uncomfortable stuff – the role played by the power dynamics that arise from a society that uplifts some from the oppression of others. If possible, consult on and resource the development of a university-wide training plan that is adapted to the specifics of localised areas of the university.

Resourcing anti-racism as a professional priority

Make anti-racism a motivator of your actions as an institution by financially investing in it as a health and wellbeing priority. Find the people who are already doing anti-racism work at your university, both work that educates on racism but also work that affirms, validates and celebrates Black communities, and other racialised communities, and ask them what they need. Develop and resource cross-sector initiatives, with your local schools and community services, to increase community access to the university, both as an educational institution and as a workplace. As suggested by Krishni Metivier (2020), 'increase funding for departments, centres and faculty that offer social justice, critical race, queer, ethnic and gender studies classes and workshops' and 'incentivize departments to hire researchers and educators who do critical race, ethnic and gender studies work', all of which can and will enhance a more equal, diverse and inclusive professionalism code and standard.

Engaging with your local community

Histories and contemporary enactment of racism are local, and universities have an obligation to the community they sit within, so reshaping ideas of 'professionalism' at your university must go hand in hand with understanding local landscapes of racism in your area, including understanding the university's role in combating and mitigating against gentrifying practices (James, 2018). 'Professionalism' in an academic context has often worked to preserve White, middle-class modes of knowledge, expertise and value, with the culture of individual HE institutions having more in common with fellow universities than the communities they are located within, while they capitalise off the 'diversity' and 'dynamism' of the area in attracting other 'professionals' to work there (Marom, 2019).

Krishni Metivier (2020) has provided a number of suggestions for how universities can better engage with their community to dismantle these practices. They are provided from within the context of the United States but are just as applicable to HE institutions in the United Kingdom. They include seeking out and ring-fencing contracts for Black, Asian and minority ethnic owned businesses through university procurement, creating low-interest loan programmes for business owners from marginalised communities, redirecting funding from law enforcement towards local restorative justice services, investing in affordable housing infrastructure in communities that are historically the target of systemic racism and offering free or low-cost community education programmes in marginalised communities.

Scrutinising your labour practices and commissioning

Evaluate the professional conditions of all your employees, and ensure all employees are being paid a living wage, beyond government minimum wage frameworks. If your cleaning services, building maintenance and/or security staff are contracted from an outsourced company, consider bringing them in-house as 'outsourced workers suffer from far worse terms and conditions than directly-employed colleagues, facing no sick pay, bare minimum holiday entitlement and meagre pensions' (Independent Workers' Union of Great Britain, 2019).

Reflective questions

- What are the frames of professionalism that have traditionally been involved with deeming something 'worth' funding, and how will you change this?[1]
- What is your understanding of the roles of 'teacher', 'student' and 'colleague' in relation to people from racialised communities?[2]
- What might be needed for these professionalism frameworks to be dismantled in an academic context, and how might academia be a powerful force in reframing them?
- If you come from a background where academic institutions have historically validated your right to be there, has this has come at the expense of people of other backgrounds?
- What role might your department play in the remaking of the university's social contract, from the idea of 'professionalism' into an explicitly anti-oppressive code of conduct?
- What is your understanding of the roles 'teacher', 'student', 'researcher' and 'subject'? What role might student activism play in reframing these roles in the context of racism?

Notes

[1] In the wake of renewed media interest in police brutality against Black communities in the United States, and globally, many HE senior management teams have put out pledges to change and make a renewed commitment to anti-racism. These issues and their solutions have been raised, campaigned for and advocated for generations, but have often been deemed disruptive and deprioritised in terms of resource allocation.

[2] Consider in your answer the ways in which your teaching and research environment have been impacted by a historical valuing of White, Western modes of knowledge, and the oppressive legacies of academia against global majority communities.

References

Akel, S. (2019) Racism and microaggressions. Insider-outsider: The role of race in shaping the experience of black and minority ethnic students. Accessed 24 July 2020, from www.gold.ac.uk/media/docs/reports/Insider-Outsider-Report-191008.pdf

Brookfield, S. (2014) Teaching our own racism: incorporating personal narratives of Whiteness into anti-racist practice. *Adult Learning*, 25(3), 89–95.

Dabiri, E. (2020) Black pupils are being wrongly excluded over their hair. I'm trying to end this discrimination. *The Guardian*. Accessed 24 July 2020, from www.theguardian.com/commentisfree/2020/feb/25/black-pupils-excluded-hair-discrimination-equality-act

Equality and Human Rights Commission (2019) *Experiences. Tackling Racial Harassment: Universities Challenged*. Accessed 24 July 2020, from www.equalityhumanrights.com/sites/default/files/tackling-racial-harassment-universities-challenged.pdf

Gray, A. (2019) The bias of 'professionalism' standards. *Stanford Social Innovation Review*. Accessed 24 July 2020, from https://ssir.org/articles/entry/the_bias_of_professionalism_standards#

Independent Workers' Union of Great Britain (2019) End outsourcing. Accessed 24 July 2020, from https://iwgb.org.uk/en/page/end-outsourcing-at-london-universities/

James, S. (2018) Universities are becoming the acceptable face of gentrification. The Independent. Accessed 24 July 2020, from www.independent.co.uk/voices/university-gentrification-ual-ucl-delancy-lendlease-acceptable-face-a8179816.html

Joseph-Salisbury, R. (2020) School policies. Race and racism in English secondary schools. Accessed 24 July 2020, from www.runnymedetrust.org/uploads/publications/pdfs/Runnymede%20Secondary%20Schools%20report%20FINAL.pdf

Kubota, R. (2019) Racism in applied linguistics literature. Confronting epistemological racism, decolonizing scholarly knowledge: race and gender in applied linguistics. Accessed 24 July 2020, from https://academic.oup.com/applij/article/doi/10.1093/applin/amz033/5519375#136839120

Marom, L. (2019) Under the cloak of professionalism: covert racism in teacher education. *Race Ethnicity and Education*, 22(3), 319–37.

Mehri, M. (2020) Anti-racism requires so much more than 'checking your privilege'. *The Guardian*. Accessed 24 July 2020, from www.theguardian.com/commentisfree/2020/jul/07/anti-racism-checking-privilege-anti-blackness

Metivier, K. (2020) Envisioning higher education as antiracist. Accessed 24 July 2020, from www.insidehighered.com/views/2020/07/02/actions-higher-ed-institutions-should-take-help-eradicate-racism-opinion

Pillay, E. (2015) Office 'professionalism' stems from structural and cultural racism. Accessed 24 July 2020, from https://gal-dem.com/office-professionalism-stems-from-structural-and-cultural-racism/

Rios, C. (2015) You call it professionalism; I call it oppression in a three-piece suit. *Everyday Feminism*. Accessed 24 July 2020, from http://everydayfeminism.com/2015/02/professionalism-and-oppression/

Rollock, N. (2019) Recommendations. Staying power: the career experiences and strategies of UK black female professors. Accessed 24 July 2020, from www.ucu.org.uk/media/10075/staying-power/pdf/ucu_rollock_february_2019.pdf

Saini, A. (2019) The disturbing return of scientific racism. Accessed 24 July 2020, from www.wired.co.uk/article/superior-the-return-of-race-science-angela-saini

Sethy, S. S. (2018) Academic ethics: teaching profession and teacher professionalism in higher education settings. *Journal of Academic Ethics*, 16(4), 287–99.

Sian, K. (2017) Teaching. Being black in a white world: Understanding racism in British universities. Accessed 24 July 2020, from http://eprints.whiterose.ac.uk/121107/1/17625_66628_1_PB.pdf.

Tate, S. A. & Page, D. (2018) Whiteliness and institutional racism: hiding behind (un)conscious bias. *Ethics and Education*, 13(1), 141–55.

UCU (University and College Union) (2016) Witness: the lived experience of UCU Black Members. Accessed 24 July 2020, from www.ucu.org.uk/media/8476/Witness-Feb-17/pdf/WITNESS_-_Voice_of_UCU_Black_Members_-_Feb_2017.pdf

Uddin, S. (2020) Racism runs deep in professional culture. Accessed 24 July 2020, from https://tulanehullabaloo.com/51652/intersections/business-professionalism-is-racist/

Van der Sluis, H., Burden, P. & Huet, I. (2017) Retrospection and reflection: the emerging influence of an institutional professional recognition scheme on professional development and academic practice in a UK university. *Innovations in Education and Teaching International*, 54(2), 126–34.

PART VII

Governance, strategy and operational systems

16

Governance and leadership

Jitesh S. B. Gajjar, Manish Maisuria and Anonymous

Introduction

There is a significant lack of Black, Asian and minority ethnic leadership in all governance systems in universities, with Black, Asian and minority ethnic staff struggling to progress to tenure and/or leadership positions. Governing bodies lack diversity with few Black, Asian and minority ethnic members, female members and those from disabled backgrounds (Advance HE, 2020a). In the context of good governance, the Framework for Supporting Governing Body Effectiveness Reviews in Higher Education (Advance HE, 2020b) recognises that diversity is a strength and is needed to avoid the 'group think' mentality seen in many governing bodies. The argument that diversity is good for business, innovation, problem solving and decision making is made in many places (as supported by Phillips, 2014 and Priest et al, 2015). Despite the Equality Act (2010), under-representation of Black, Asian and minority ethnic staff at senior levels in governance, leadership positions and decision-making bodies (that is, Universities UK, Office for Students) is well documented (Advance HE, 2018; 2020c), with Black, Asian and minority ethnic staff struggling to progress to tenure and leadership positions in universities (Weale, 2019).

Bhopal and Henderson (2019) have identified that the Athena Swan Charter (ASC) and the REC influence policy making, governance and leadership of awards. They argue that the ASC mostly benefits White, middle-class women, setting a covertly higher precedence on gender issues above race inequality, which has resulted 'in a hierarchy of oppression in which women's experiences have been privileged over [the intersection] of men and women of colour' (Bhopal, 2021). Bhopal and Henderson (2019) argue that gender equality is progressing because the ASC process has become more established and embedded in HEIs over the last 20 years in contrast to the REC, which was formed only in 2016. The charters do recognise and address issues pertaining to governance and offer frameworks for change in different institutions; however, there is still a need to understand how sustainable and efficacious changes to governance are made. When critically reflecting on the role of such equalities frameworks, researchers like Hu-DeHart (2000) argue that policies for diversity and inclusion are 'camouflage for the self-interest, power and privilege of dominant groups'. See also Iverson (2007) and Lehan, Hussey and Babcock (2020), who studied equality and diversity practice in universities and educational institutions in the United States.

HE policies are critical to transforming governance and leadership in HE (Wise, Dickinson, Katan & Gallegos, 2020). Bhopal and Pitkin (2020) considered the impact of the REC on policies in HE, and despite the call for Critical Race Theory to be utilised to address the perpetuation of racism in HE structures and policy, it is met with resistance (for example, Doharty, Madriaga & Joseph-Salisbury, 2020).

Many governance and leadership structures need to shift from their legislative requirements to a moral and ethical duty to change the embedded racist practices and beliefs that reinforce the interests of small elite groups typically held in leadership and governance (Bhopal, 2014; Harper, 2017). As noted by Ahmed (2007), strategy documents and diligent marketing can project HEIs into being institutions that embrace diversity, but in many cases, they serve to conceal racism and obstruct real progress.

Voice of the author

I have been in the university system for 35 years and a member of the Senate on two occasions. The Senate is the main body with academic representation, responsible for academic policies, regulations and other matters. I have been a member of many university and faculty committees responsible for various aspects of social responsibility, EDI and widening participation. I have sat on the promotions panel and was on a select group with the head of department and heads of groups, discussing day-to-day management. On a personal level, if asked if I have experienced overt racism, I would have to say no. However, there have been many occasions when I have felt that I have been treated differently to other (White) colleagues, certainly in matters to do with workload, responsibilities, equal pay and career progression.

There are many stories one can share that demonstrate how governance and leadership operate with regard to Black, Asian and minority ethnic matters and EDI within my institution. As a member of the Senate, I have observed that EDI matters have never come up for discussion as an agenda item in any of the meetings that I have attended. One of my colleagues who is a Black, Asian and minority ethnic member and who was a member of the Board of Governors (BoG) echoes a similar experience with respect to the BoG. The BoG and Senate are the two principal authorities responsible for governance and policy matters in the university and how it operates. The BoG can hold the senior leadership team to account with respect to key performance indicators and targets and goals, but when many members and the chair are chosen/nominated by a few people at the very top, the BoG is not viewed as being fully independent. In my institution, one of the largest universities in Europe, there has been very little change in the last five to ten years with respect to Black, Asian and minority ethnic people holding senior positions within the organisation. The few Black, Asian and minority ethnic committee members are either token appointments or seen as figureheads. On the other hand, however, it is very noticeable that the gender balance has improved considerably at the highest levels.

In my faculty (and others) the few Black, Asian and minority ethnic staff that have leadership-type roles are kept at bay and if any voice strong opinions, which run counter to what the senior leadership team think, highlight how they are further marginalised. Black, Asian and minority ethnic staff in these roles have personal and other dilemmas in that they are the few such people to hold those posts, but part of their salaries is paid by the centre. As such, they feel they are not allowed 'to bite the hand feeding them'. With such token appointments, the centre has a process to mute any dissent and criticisms of shortcomings of the senior leadership. In fact, the Black, Asian and minority ethnic staff feel they have to take part in the collective decision-making process of the senior leadership team and sit out uncomfortable moments. For example, when prestigious fellowships were advertised, the process for shortlisting candidates was interfered with by very senior staff even though the shortlisting committee involving Black, Asian and minority ethnic and other members had made their choices. I too have witnessed such interference in a shortlisting committee meeting when a candidate, who was not on anyone else's shortlist, had to be discussed because the dean wanted that candidate. When you point out the biases and flaws in these types of events, you are not invited to sit on any more such meetings. On one occasion, I directly pointed out discriminatory practices in the recruitment of postgraduate research students, which were adversely affecting students from a Middle Eastern country. The person responsible for introducing such discriminatory practices now occupies an even higher and more influential role in the department. The very same person was also accused of discrimination by an overseas student but cleared. At another meeting I suggested that staff on appointment panels need to do unconscious bias (UB) training. The then chair of the ASC raised objections and said, "surely you are not going to subject us to all that UB nonsense". That person is now our Head of Department. (Admittedly, the unconscious bias training that we get asked to do has been a big issue as well as it is perceived as being very company and business focused and not of much relevance to academia. When staff come out of UB training and think they are not biased, you know there is a problem.) I have seen the impact of unfair comments made by a senior member of staff on the promotion panel, who had not completed the required mandatory UB training, destroy the case of one Black, Asian and minority ethnic member of staff.

On one occasion I was interviewing with the Head of Department administration for a part-time post for which I had some grant money. Two people were shortlisted; one was a Black, Asian and minority ethnic woman more qualified than the other candidate for the post. I chose the Black, Asian and minority ethnic woman; my colleague chose the other candidate. I would not change my position, and neither would my colleague. We agreed that the interviews should occur again with another independent person present. The next day I was informed by my colleague that the Black, Asian and minority ethnic candidate had withdrawn their application. The successful candidate was of course well known to my colleague and may well have been promised the post in advance.

Change domains

Making equality, diversity, inclusion and accessibility a standing item

EDI incorporating anti-racism should be a mandatory item in governing bodies at least once a year (as a sole agenda item). Senior leadership teams need to be adequately challenged on their action plans and the actions subsequently implemented. We suggest that membership of mechanisms like the BoG are to include external experts from governing bodies. EDI should not be the last item on the agenda to be glossed over without any discussion because meetings are running late. Independent scrutiny of senior leadership teams is needed, and difficult questions need to be asked by people of colour who continuously live through the issues and are expected to provide significant labour to facilitate change within HEIs.

Governing bodies co-creating a league table

There is evidence that suggests featuring low on league tables can prompt behavioural changes (Sauder & Espeland, 2009; Goglio, 2016). Low-ranking HEIs can cause reputational and brand damage that can affect income and even recruiting of the best talents (Johnes, 2018). A co-created model of rankings and leagues created by the sector could be a prime opportunity for the sector to monitor their performance and hold themselves to account where they have fallen short.

Governance structures and leadership sponsoring race equality activities

Activities that enhance the experience of Black, Asian and minority ethnic staff and students (with respect to intersectionality) should have full support and sponsorship from senior leaders. A co-designed structure needs to be in place that allows for transparent feedback loops and dialogue from the university frontlines all the way up to the senior leaders within an HE institution, and engaging with Black, Asian and minority ethnic staff through networks and events can enable feedback from EDI staff upwards.

Black, Asian and minority ethnic staff forums

These spaces for Black, Asian and minority ethnic staff and students should be developed, maintained and occur regularly to ensure the staff and student voices are encouraged to speak out, represented in university strategic committees to ensure there is adequate representation to give assurance that issues are raised and addressed through purposive action. All HE institutions should have a space for Black, Asian and minority ethnic staff to engage, discuss and share experiences with safe sponsorship from a senior leader. This sponsorship should require a senior leader to ensure they actively share issues concerning the racial landscape of the institution while considering opportunities to alleviate barriers to accelerate change.

Race equality action committees

Race equality action committees should be embedded, chaired and sponsored by senior leaders and an academic lead, addressing and collating issues presented from Black, Asian and minority ethnic staff forums to feed into higher EDI committee(s) to support the design of meaningful and authentic diversity and inclusion interventions and programmes. Membership of an action group should include representation from across the university and students' union and/or association. Black, Asian and minority ethnic student groups, whether as part of a students' union and/or association, should have a senior leadership sponsor to ensure that the views and voices of Black, Asian and minority ethnic students are embedded into governance structures and leaders' decision making.

Relevant union representatives should be involved in Black, Asian and minority ethnic related groups. This is imperative to developing a critical relationship with the union and ensuring authentic and trustworthy monitoring and impact of Black, Asian and minority ethnic related activity, EDI policy development and the effective inclusion and involvement of Black, Asian and minority ethnic staff voices across all grades and levels to enhance staff and student experience.

Reflective questions

- What are members of the senior leadership team actively doing to demonstrate their support and allyship to the race agenda?
- How are you ensuring the staff body is involved in university-wide discussions on race?
- For the number of staff that have been on leadership programmes (for example STELLAR HE), why have they not progressed to leadership roles within your institution?
- Why is there a differential pay gap for Black, Asian and minority ethnic staff that are paid less for doing the same role as their White counterparts? What measures are in place to begin to address the inequalities and what is the time frame?
- How will you improve your EDI data infrastructure to ensure senior leaders and governing boards and committees can make high-quality, evidence-informed decisions?
- Do you anticipate any further public statement being made following the BLM events of 2020 to demonstrate your commitment to becoming an anti-racist institution?[1]

- As senior leaders, how will you translate your commitments into effective, authentic and meaningful action?
- In your position of authority, EDI continues to be housed with HR but this is highly ineffective to institutional change – what will you do to change this?
- What are the timescales for improving Black, Asian and minority ethnic representation at senior levels of internal decision-making bodies (that is, EDI committees), and what are the consequences for not tackling racism?
- Can you explain why EDI and accessibility are not recurring agenda items at Senate and BoG meetings?
- What is being undertaken to govern a more inclusive curriculum that may be called 'decolonised'?
- What actions are you undertaking to ensure two-way communications between Black, Asian and minority ethnic support staff and the university?
- How is the student body involved in university-wide discussions on race?

Note

[1] As an institution it could be perceived as cynical to issue a message shortly after the death of a Black life about your institution being diverse, not tolerating racism and condemning violence when no progress has been made in previous years about matters affecting Black, Asian and minority ethnic staff and students. For instance, demonstrating accountability in failures concerning the discrimination that Black, Asian and minority ethnic staff face at work, in securing career progression or the degree-awarding gap.

References

Advance HE (2018) Equality in higher education: statistical report 2018. Accessed 26 July 2020, from https://www.advance-he.ac.uk/knowledge-hub/equality-higher-education-statistical-report-2018

Advance HE (2020a) Governance in higher education: understanding governance performance and future challenges. Accessed 6 August 2020, from www.advance-he.ac.uk/knowledge-hub/governance-higher-education-understanding-governance-performance-and-future

Advance HE (2020b) Governing body effectiveness. Accessed 6 August 2020, from www.advance-he.ac.uk/guidance/governance/governing-body-effectiveness

Advance HE (2020c) Statistics reports. Accessed 6 August 2020, form www.advance-he.ac.uk/guidance/equality-diversity-and-inclusion/using-data-and-evidence/statistics-reports

Ahmed, S. (2007) 'You end up doing the document rather than doing the doing': diversity, race equality and the politics of documentation. *Ethnic and Racial Studies*, 30(4), 590–609. DOI: 10.1080/01419870701356015.

Bhopal, K. (2014) The experiences of BME academics in higher education: aspirations in the face of inequality. *Leadership Foundation for Higher Education Stimulus Papers*, ISBN 978-1-906627-70-6.

Bhopal, K. (2021) White female academics are being privileged above women – and men – of colour. *The Guardian Higher Education*. Accessed 20 November 2021, from www.theguardian.com/education/2020/jul/28/uks-white-female-academics-are-being-privileged-above-women-and-men-of-colour

Bhopal, K. & Henderson, H. (2019) Competing inequalities: gender versus race in higher education institutions in the UK. *Educational Review*, 73(2), 153–169. DOI: 10.1080/00131911.2019.1642305.

Bhopal, K. & Pitkin, C. (2020) 'Same old story, just a different policy': race and policy making in higher education in the UK. *Race Ethnicity and Education*, 23(4), 530–47. DOI: 10.1080/13613324.2020.1718082.

Claeys-Kulik, A. L., Jørgensen, T. E. & Stöber, H. (2019) *Diversity, Equity and Inclusion in European Higher Education Institutions: Results from the INVITED Project*. Brussels and Geneva: European University Association.

Doharty, N., Madriaga, M. & Joseph-Salisbury, R. (2020) The university went to 'decolonise' and all they brought back was lousy diversity double-speak! Critical race counter-stories from faculty of colour in 'decolonial' times. *Educational Philosophy and Theory*, 53(3), 1–12.

Goglio, V. (2016) One size fits all? A different perspective on university rankings. *Journal of Higher Education Policy and Management*, 38(2), 212–26. DOI: 10.1080/1360080x.2016.1150553.

Harper, S. R. (2017) Racially responsive leadership: addressing the longstanding problem of racism in higher education. In *Challenges in Higher Education Leadership* (pp 145–56). New York: Routledge.

Hu-DeHart, E. (2000) The diversity project: institutionalizing multiculturalism or managing differences? *Academe*, 86(5), 38. DOI: 10.2307/40251919.

Iverson, S. V. (2007) Camouflaging power and privilege: a critical race analysis of university diversity policies. *Educational Administration Quarterly*, 43(5), 586–611. DOI: 10.1177/0013161x07307794.

Johnes, J. (2018) University rankings: what do they really show? *Scientometrics*, 115(1), 585–606.

Lehan, T., Hussey, H. & Babcock, A. (2020) Mission unaccomplished: beyond 'talk[ing] a good game' to promote diversity and inclusion. *Journal of Educational Research and Practice*, 10(1), 12. DOI: 10.5590/JERAP.2020.10.1.12.

Mirza, H. S. (2018) Racism in higher education: 'What then, can be done?'. In *Dismantling Race in Higher Education* (pp 3–23). Cham: Palgrave Macmillan.

Ntim, C. G., Soobaroyen, T. & Broad, M. J. (2017) Governance structures, voluntary disclosures and public accountability: the case of UK higher education institutions. *Accounting, Auditing & Accountability Journal*, 30(1), 65–118.

Phillips, K. W. (2014) How diversity works. *Scientific American*, 311(4), 42–7. DOI: /10.1038/scientificamerican1014-42.

Priest, N., Esmail, A., Kline, R., Rao, M., Coghill, Y. & Williams, D. R. (2015) Promoting equality for ethnic minority NHS staff--what works? *BMJ (Clinical Research Ed.)*, 351, h3297. DOI: 10.1136/bmj.h3297.

Sauder, M. & Espeland, W. N. (2009) The discipline of rankings: tight coupling and organizational change. *American Sociological Review*, 74(1), 63–82. DOI: 10.1177/000312240907400104.

Weale, S. (2019) UK universities' BME staff less likely to hold top jobs. *The Guardian*. Accessed 6 July 2020, from www.theguardian.com/education/2019/oct/15/uk-universities-bme-staff-less-likely-to-hold-top-jobs

Wise, G., Dickinson, C., Katan, T. & Gallegos, M. C. (2020) Inclusive higher education governance: managing stakeholders, strategy, structure and function. *Studies in Higher Education*, 45(2), 339–52.

17

Operations and processes

Manvir Kaur Grewal

Introduction

The neoliberal universities' attempt at modernity does not extend to examining the Whiteness of academia and how it is sustained in the positions of leadership. The continuous quest for more data and statistics shows the focus has been proving the problem of racism exists instead of exploring what structures are in place that allow the domination of White leadership and the absence of racially minoritised leaders. Although universities are keen to engage in performative activism, little is done to examine White privilege in a meaningful way. The implementation of anti-racism, specifically the advancement of racially minoritised individuals, specifically Black leaders into leadership roles, is rare across the sector (UCU, 2019).

Reporting issues of racism is problematic; racially minoritised staff and students are often inadvertently identified if instances of racism are reported to manager staff in universities (Arday, 2018). This theme focuses on issues pertaining to reporting and processes for empowering racially minoritised staff to report racism in the university setting. Despite grand and generic pledges of anti-racism, little has been done to advance the significant lack of racially minoritised leaders in the universities' governance, operations and systems (Arday & Wilson, 2021).

There is clear evidence of significant under-representation of racially minoritised staff Black, Asian and minority ethnic staff at all senior levels and operations in academia (Ahmed, 2012; Bhopal & Brown, 2016; ECU, 2015; Tate & Bagguley, 2017; HESA, 2016). As of the 2018/19 academic year, among academic staff, 475 managers, directors and senior officials identify as White, compared with 15 senior leaders who identify as Asian and none who identify as Black (HESA, 2020). A similar trend follows non-academic staff, with 10,510 managers, directors and senior officials identifying as White, compared with the disproportionate 410 who identify as Asian and 185 who identify as Black (HESA, 2020). Most of the racial justice work involves gathering the data, which Allen (2020) argues that

> data will provide evidence of the problem and help you identify where race inequality is manifesting but there will always be too much and not enough … knowing when to dig deep and when to see the bigger picture will help you spot the patterns and trends because the data will not join the dots for itself.

The focus must now be on creating actionable points from these statistics (Advance HE, 2020).

To counteract this under-representation, HE has created targeted initiatives focusing solely on diversity and equality (Mirza, 2017). However, institutions reflect a slow increase of racially minoritised staff in leadership and governance structures (ECU, 2015; Bhopal & Brown, 2016). Commitment and initiatives of diversity and equality in leadership, operations and governance must move beyond pledges of intent and look to dismantle the culture and space of academia (Ahmed, 2012; Mulcahy, 2011). Current equality initiatives conflate concepts of gender and race, leaving little room for intersectional analysis (Bhopal & Henderson, 2019). Utilising intersectional analyses would move past 'talking the talk' of diversity, which does little to address the culture that keeps racially minoritised individuals, specifically Black staff, absent in governance and leadership (Healy, Kirton & Noon, 2011).

The governance and leadership structures of HE demonstrate an overwhelming presence of White people, which is the clearest indictment of unequal practices (Mirza, 2017). A lack of representation means White people yield enormous amounts of power in decision making (Ahmed, 2012; Mirza, 2017). The Whiteness of academia has been advanced by White, male canons, pushing a Eurocentric patriarchal perception of leadership qualities (Ahmed, 2012; Pilkington, 2013). Racially minoritised academics have little energy to challenge inequitable cultures and practices as much of their efforts focus on how to navigate and survive the academy because of racial microaggressions and inequities (Arday, 2018). As such, racially minoritised staff are often perceived as unable to successfully lead, govern and strategise (Arday, 2018). White allies have a responsibility to use their privilege to disrupt White spaces to endorse the promotion and career progression of all academics in leadership roles (Miller, 2016).

This literature indicates the need for a change in the operations and practices of HE to truly advance racially minoritised staff in enhancing their performance and success in the academy (Coco Khan, 2017). HEIs are tentative and complacent in systemic racism as they repeatedly cultivate unequal cultures, requiring people of colour to navigate White spaces as a condition of their existence (Trevethan, 2020). This rapid review has shown that there needs to be a cultural and institutional shift in how racially minoritised staff and students perceive HE, in enhancing its operational capacity and the role of White allies to provide opportunities for racially minoritised colleagues to pursue leadership trajectories.

The increasing racial tensions, from the murder of George Floyd in 2020, coupled with the disproportionate impact of COVID-19 on ethnic minority groups has amplified the discussion on anti-racism in HE and the spotlight once again has shone on who has decision-making powers. Now more than ever, HE sees an urgency to re-examine its operational and legal commitments under the Equality Act 2010 and to eliminate the institutional policies and processes that internalise racism and hinder racially minoritised staff from holding senior leadership positions. In response, universities came out in droves with official statements, five-year commitment plans, commitments to diversify and decolonise, enhancing equality and diversity as well as creating resources and reading lists to prompt anti-racism actions. Yet, there was little focus on advancing racially minoritised staff into leadership roles.

Voice of the author

A substantial amount of work on equality and diversity falls on racially minoritised individuals who are often sitting at the intersection of other minoritised identities, and in most cases, it is a bottom–up approach. Often, we are asked to forsake our wellbeing and do the work of diversity on top of our role with no increase in hours or work allocation. Doing the groundwork can be rewarding but it seems reductive that those in leadership and governance positions, who are tasked to maximise the impact of decision making across the HE landscape, come from predominantly White and elite backgrounds. Those in power do not implement the generic pledges of equality and diversity; it then becomes solely the responsibility of minoritised individuals.

Being a Punjabi woman in a White space is complex. It does little to acknowledge the emotional labour that is experienced while navigating the fluidity of racism. I yield little decision-making authority in a space that historically is contingent on White power and no matter how many generic pledges or grand gestures come from the top, a lack of representation equates to a lack of culture change. Without a change in the culture, a transformation of the way the system works, a review of who remains present and who is absent, the systems of oppression will remain. My attempts to disrupt the White space can feel futile and add to feelings of 'othering'. A lack of intersectional analysis of oppressive structures means we are fighting on more than one front, while constantly encountering racial microaggressions and routinely being attacked by imposter syndrome.

The people that sit on recruitment and selection panels decide our progression and if that space remains occupied by Whiteness, the criteria to assess suitability speaks to the needs, expectations and behavioural cues built out of those all-White contexts. Universities must ensure visible representation of racially minoritised colleagues, paying particular attention to those who sit on the intersect of multiple identities on these panels. A commitment to visible representation in leadership and governance creates the pathway to our voices and experiences being noticed and recognised as value-laden. The White insiders often proclaim to be our 'allies' yet I find they are often complicit in maintaining the status quo. Although they have the power to influence the shift of hierarchical structures, often allyship becomes performative and is misconceived as a permanent designation. The work of allyship is well intentioned but often recentres Whiteness (Tuck & Yang, 2012) and advances the White saviour complex. If allyship was thought of more critically we could progressively unfold towards a greater embodiment of anti-racism, one that dismantles a system that oppresses us as opposed to dismantling ourselves to fit into a system that continues to oppress us.

Change domains

Acknowledging Whiteness in operations

Start by acknowledging the Whiteness of the academy and operational structures.

One way to acknowledge Whiteness in these structures is to examine how overwhelmingly White they are and push for visible diversity. Visibility demands that minoritised individuals remain in the room, that their stories, perspectives and experiences are visible. This can be done by engaging in positive action practices and processes. Institutions should be pushed to commit to increased representation in all recruitment and selection panels, including informal groups and committees. UCL developed a fair recruitment specialist initiative that acknowledges that recruitment panels often discriminate against candidates due to their ethnicity and have created a pool of trained specialists to bring visible diversity to panels (UCL, 2020).

Radical reverse mentoring

Implement radical reverse mentoring processes and schemes that provide opportunities for continuing professional development that safeguard the mentor, while ensuring there is a clear and even distribution of power and purpose in such programmes. Reverse mentoring schemes are those that see senior colleagues being mentored by junior colleagues (Murphy, 2012; Kaše, Saksida & Mihelič, 2018). Evidence shows they can enhance culture change and disrupt traditional power structures that perpetuate systemic racism (Murphy, 2012). This can be done by creating a pool of racially minoritised role models at senior and junior levels and having them mentor senior staff. This not only identifies our very capable colleagues from varying backgrounds and intersect that we know already exist to carry out leadership roles (Mirza, 2017), but it speaks to the lived experience of racially minoritised academics. It also makes room for endorsement from White colleagues, otherwise known as White sanction (Miller, 2016), which in and of itself can be a powerful attempt to enhance professional development and promote diversity.

Meaningful life-long learning and operational development

Organise dedicated equality and diversity training that explores intersectionality and the fallacy of a post-racial or a colour-blind society. Much of the work of unconscious or implicit bias training is wholly ineffective, given online and largely a box-ticking exercise, making it non-actionable and obsolete (as noted in Atweologun, Cornish & Tresh, 2018). Instead, we must advocate for training that requires us to examine how White supremacy and ideals function in operational spaces, focusing on approaches to improvement, employee performance and resourcing. More critical and contemporary training allows institutions and senior leaders to enhance their racial literacy and disrupt neoliberal logics. This also places further emphasis on changing the system and the ideas and perceptions of leadership as opposed to changing racially minoritised colleagues into a predetermined mould of leadership, which has developed out of an all-White context.

Staff networks building continuing partnerships

Generally, staff networks can be a powerful tool for empowering equality groups, supporting staff and an avenue for advice and consultation as business operations seek models for continuous improvement. The power of staff networks ought to be amplified; consider creating staff networks that speak to each other and work together to develop intersectional approaches to equality and diversity across different identities. Evidence shows that progression and promotion, formal and informal processes, are very much linked to networking. Create more spaces that work in collaboration across university levels to ensure that operational processes and policies are not reinventing the wheel but complimenting one another.

Intersectionality and operations

All actions and reforms should be spearheaded utilising intersectionality to understand how overlapping forms of identity impact or act as a barrier to promoting racially minoritised colleagues to leadership roles. This must be done with caution and with experts who engage with intersectional analysis, so as to go beyond the colour-blind intersectionality and gender-blind intersectionality, thereby 'further naturalizing White male heterosexuality as the normative baseline' (Carbado, 2013). Using an intersectional prism gives us a better chance of understanding colleagues and students through their lived experiences (Bagilhole, 2010). By doing this we can explore how power and privilege intersect (Atewologun, Sealy & Vinnicombe, 2015), and find new ways to action diversity and equality measures to move away from non-actionable, tokenistic and obsolete singular measures.

Reflective questions

- Do you have visible diversity in operations, processes and policies? If so, how does this operate?
- When looking at improvement and implementation models, how are you integrating the views and experiences of racially minoritised staff?
- How is diversity and inclusion represented in your operational values?
- How do you hold senior leaders accountable for equality and diversity initiatives and operations plans?
- Does your operations plan consider racially minoritised staff when thinking about measures of performance and success?
- What kinds of learning and operations programmes/ training are in place to understand concepts such as allyship, White privilege?

- How are procurement processes and policies enabling of EDI? How do we assess who we partner with?
- How important is it for you to see minoritised staff, specifically those who sit on the intersection of varying identities, represented in all operational processes and systems?

References

Advance HE (2019) Equality in higher education: statistical report 2019. Accessed 17 August 2020, from www.advance-he.ac.uk/knowledge-hub/equality-higher-education-statistical-report-2019

Advance HE (2020) Collecting equality data. Accessed 30 December 2020, from www.advance-he.ac.uk/guidance/equality-diversity-and-inclusion/using-data-and-evidence/collecting-equality-data#Related-publications

Ahmed, S. (2012) *On Being Included: Racism and Diversity in Institutional Life*. Durham, NC: Duke University Press.

Allen, S. (2020) Racial justice at work, from gestures to action. Accessed 17 August 2020, from https://vergemagazine.co.uk/racial-justice-at-work-from-gestures-to-action/

Arday, J. (2018) Understanding race and educational leadership in higher education: exploring the black and ethnic minority (BME) experience. *Management in Education*, 32(4), 192–200. DOI: 10.1177/0892020618791002.

Arday, J. & Wilson, M. (2021). Many rivers to cross: the challenges and barriers facing aspiring black, Asian and minority ethnic (BAME) leaders in the academy. In *Doing Equity and Diversity for Success in Higher Education* (pp 313–24). Cham: Palgrave Macmillan.

Atewologun, D., Sealy, R. & Vinnicombe, S. (2015) Revealing intersectional dynamics in organizations: introducing 'intersectional identity work'. *Gender, Work & Organization*, 23(3), 223–47. DOI: 10.1111/gwao.12082.

Atewologun, D., Cornish, T. & Tresh, F. (2018) Unconscious bias training. An assessment of the evidence for effectiveness. *Equality and Human Rights Commission Research Report*, 113. Accessed 17 August 2020, from www.equalityhumanrights.com/en/publication-download/unconscious-bias-training-assessment-evidence-effectiveness.

Bagilhole, B. (2010) Applying the lens of intersectionality to UK equal opportunities and diversity policies. *Canadian Journal of Administrative Sciences / Revue Canadienne Des Sciences de l'Administration*, 27(3), 263–71. DOI: 10.1002/cjas.167.

Bhopal, K. & Brown, H. (2016) Black and minority ethnic leaders: support networks and strategies for success in higher education. Accessed 17 August 2020, from https://www.advance-he.ac.uk/knowledge-hub/black-and-minority-ethnic-leaders-support-networks-and-strategies-success-higher

Bhopal, K. & Henderson, H. (2019) Competing inequalities: gender versus race in higher education institutions in the UK. *Educational Review*, 73(2), 153–169.

Carbado, D. W. (2013) Colorblind intersectionality. *Signs: Journal of Women in Culture and Society*, 38(4), 811–45. DOI: 10.1086/669666.

Coco Khan (2017) Do universities have a problem with promoting their Black, Asian and minority ethnic staff? *The Guardian.* Accessed 30 December 2020, from www.theguardian.com/higher-education-network/2017/nov/16/do-universities-have-a-problem-with-promoting-their-Black,Asian and minority ethnic-staff

ECU (Equality Challenge Unit) (2015) Equality in higher education: statistical report. Accessed 16 August 2020, from www.ecu.ac.uk/publications/equality-higher-education-statistical-report-2015

Equality Act (2010) Accessed 1 January 2021, from www.legislation.gov.uk/ukpga/2010/15/contents

Healy, G., Kirton, G. & Noon, M. (2011) *Equality, Inequalities and Diversity* (pp 1–17). London: Red Globe Press.

HESA (2016) Staff in higher education 2015/16. Accessed 17 August 2020, from www.hesa.ac.uk/data-and-analysis/publications/staff-2015-16

HESA (2020) Higher education staff satistics: UK, 2018/19. Accessed 16 August 2020, from www.hesa.ac.uk/news/23-01-2020/sb256-higher-education-staff-statistics

Humphreys, S. (2010) The Equality Act 2010. *Research Ethics*, 6(3), 95. DOI: 10.1177/174701611000600306.

Kaše, R., Saksida, T. & Mihelič, K. K. (2018) Skill development in reverse mentoring: motivational processes of mentors and learners. *Human Resource Management*, 58(1), 57–69. DOI: 10.1002/hrm.21932

Miller, P. (2016) 'White sanction', institutional, group and individual interaction in the promotion and progression of black and minority ethnic academics and teachers in England. *Power and Education*, 8(3), 205–21. DOI: 10.1177/1757743816672880.

Mirza, H. S (2017) 'One in a million': a journey of a post-colonial woman of colour in the White academy. In D. Gabriel and S. A. Tate (eds) (pp 39–54) *Inside the Ivory Tower: Narratives of Women of Colour Surviving and Thriving in British Academia*. London: UCL IOE Press.

Mulcahy, L. (2011) *Legal Architecture*. London: Routledge.

Murphy, W. M. (2012) Reverse mentoring at work: fostering cross-generational learning and developing millennial leaders. *Human Resource Management*, 51(4), 549–73. DOI: 10.1002/hrm.21489.

Pilkington, A. (2013) The interacting dynamics of institutional racism in higher education. *Race Ethnicity and Education*, 16(2), 225–45. DOI: 10.1080/13613324.2011.646255.

Tate, S. A. & Bagguley, P. (2017) Building the anti-racist university: next steps. *Race Ethnicity and Education*, 20(3), 289–99. DOI: 10.1080/13613324.2016.1260227.

Trevethan, G. (2020) Black bodies in white spaces: how can we be what we can't see? Accessed 30 December 2020, from https://students.brunel.ac.uk/campus-news/black-bodies-in-White-spaces-how-can-we-be-what-we-cant-see

Tuck, E. & Yang, K.W. (2012) Decolonization is not a metaphor. *Decolonization: Indigeneity, Education and Society*, 1(1), 1–40.

UCL (2020) Fair recruitment specialist initiative. Accessed 18 August 2020, from www.ucl.ac.uk/equality-diversity-inclusion/equality-areas/race-equality/fair-recruitment-specialist-initiative

UCU (University and College Union) (2019) Black academic staff face double whammy in promotion and pay stakes. Accessed 30 December 2020, from www.ucu.org.uk/article/10360/Black-academic-staff-face-double-whammy-in-promotion-and-pay-stakes

18

Strategy, planning and accountability

Shaminder Takhar, Rashid Aziz, Musharrat J. Ahmed-Landeryou and Pamela Thomas

Introduction

University equality and diversity policy and strategies are at high risk of becoming quickly obsolete and unactionable in their relevance, solutions and implementation (a theme noted in Bhopal & Pitkin, 2020). Commitments have been made since the implementation of the Equality Act 2010. This area of interrogation highlights actions that can be made to ensure that all equality and diversity strategies are embedded with intersectionality at the heart of their development.

Wilkinson and Picket's book *The Spirit Level* (2009) showed evidence of the levels of inequality experienced in the US and triggered a debate in the UK where the Equality Act was passed in 2010. To comply with legal requirements regarding discriminatory practices, HEIs were obliged to produce policies on good practice in a range of areas including processes of recruitment and appointment (ECU, 2012). Universities commit themselves to EDI issues as a result of legislation. However, this leads to promoting ideas about achieving one's potential, and presenting themselves as meritocratic (Crozier, 2018). Research has shown a different kind of story. The symbolic commitment to diversity is revealed in Sara Ahmed's findings in her book, *On Being Included* (2012). It demonstrates how diversity has been institutionalised in universities, where Whiteness and privilege conceal how racism operates and resistance to change regarding equality is expressed as a 'brick wall'. The injustice experienced in neoliberal societies is replicated in universities and is central in Danny Dorling's *Injustice* (2021), June Sarpong's *Diversify* (2017), Kalwant Bhopal's *White Privilege* (2018), and Nicola Rollock's, Staying Power (2019). Scientifically speaking, people of colour are told that there are minimal differences between races (Saini, 2021; Rutherford, 2020). However, Black, Asian and minority ethnic academic staff continue to experience discrimination and exclusion exemplified by the small number of Black, Asian and minority ethnic staff at professorial level (Bhopal & Jackson, 2013; Bhopal, 2014; 2015; Arday, 2015). In 2017–18, Black, Asian and minority ethnic staff progression stood at 13 per cent and universities began to investigate the barriers through collaboration between leaders, staff and student unions (LFHE, 2017; SOAS, 2018). With reference to students, an attainment awarding gap between White and minority ethnic students continues to persist (Berry & Loke, 2011; Singh, 2011; HEA, 2012; Stevenson, 2012; ; Richardson, 2018).

The role of staff networks is important to champion equality and diversity issues of Black, Asian and minority ethnic staff, as it represents their views and provides a collective voice to achieve positive change (Inko-Tariah, 2015). Networks provide social and professional networking opportunities to increase wellbeing and community engagement and can often offer a confidential and safe space for discussions on racial inequalities demonstrated in the workplace (Bhopal, Brown & Jackson, 2018). Furthermore, networks can be instrumental in shaping the EDI policy of a university through consultation and collaboration on strategy, policy and practice and in providing guidance on race issues (Colgan & McKearney, 2012; Denard Thomas et al, 2015). Importantly, a staff network does not operate without a network sponsor who champions the racial inequalities that exist within an institution. It is important to identify such a person who is willing to take up the challenge to stamp out the inequalities that exist (Akinbosede, 2020). However, this can present its own challenges, for example, finding someone suitable on the senior management team who will understand the issues and be willing to be responsible and accountable to the cause (Ashong-Lamptey, 2016; Jeito Consulting, 2017). Training for senior management, executives and Boards of Governors who lead our universities is not only critical but crucial to progress anti-racism in the university, particularly when the executive is usually male and White (Arday, 2018).

There are many courses available on diversity training, including active bystander and inclusive leadership training, and unconscious/implicit bias training, which have had mixed reactions regarding their effectiveness (Easterly & Ricard, 2011; Noon, 2018). Creating awareness of race issues and the centrality of Whiteness is important and noted in *White Fragility*, where Robin DiAngelo (as cited by Iqbal, 2019) states that 'racism is a White problem. It was constructed and created by White people and the ultimate responsibility lies with White people'. Claiming responsibility and, in the words of Angela Davis, becoming 'anti-racist' is better than being a non-racist or neutral or colour-blind. The move towards anti-racism is a journey through which a world view is developed that does not view Black people as a social problem or deficient. At that point racial equality at the intersections of gender, sexuality, class and disability looks desirable and not a demand (Welton, Diem & Carpenter, 2019). It means the focus must be on the exercising of power, allyship and working towards effective and meaningful policy change (Imperial College London, 2020).

The biggest question for HEIs is how to meaningfully scaffold cultural change action work to productively eliminate systemic racism (Case and Ngo, 2017). For any institution to become an anti-racist institution, more is needed than just policies, procedures and unconscious bias training. Often, these policies are inadequate, disjointed and a superfluous requirement to enact compulsory training that becomes a tick-box exercise, that has yet to show meaningful and impactful change (Atewologun et al, 2018; Stevens, 2020). What is required is a whole institutional approach to anti-racism, with related impactful actions that show responsibility in changing, monitoring and reviewing cultural change and to further adapt and continue to check if the organisation is still fit for anti-racist purpose (Kalev et al, 2006). This will show explicit accountability through these actions and send a clear and strong message of intolerance of racism. This starts with the leadership being engaged, authentic and compassionate (Kline, 2020).

Any changes to strategies, action plans and accountability measures need to align with anti-racism principles and practices, which should bring about disrupting and dismantling systemic racism so that staff and students start from a level playing field with their White peers. All must thrive and make their own opportunities without the extra burden of navigating the hurdles of racism. Therefore, designing policies and practices that are equitable for those who deliver and receive the services will be a benefit to all (Bhopal & Henderson, 2019).

The changes required to be implemented are multifactorial and have multiple perspectives due to the complex construct of racism and being anti-racist. In order for change to be meaningful, impactful and a game changer for any HEI, we must make the right start; if not, it is possible 'to go everywhere and end up nowhere', which is no longer an option.

Voice of the author

The continuing Black, Asian and minority ethnic attainment awarding gap is a consequence of institutional racism. The Black, Asian and minority ethnic attainment awarding gap is described as the proportion of Black, Asian and minority ethnic students achieving a first or 2:1 degree compared with their White counterparts (Universities UK and the National Union of Students, 2019). Maybe it is time to change the thinking, which will reframe the institutions' actions to be anti-racist. For Black, Asian and minority ethnic students to continue to hear that the gap continues is counterproductive; students have voiced that by hearing about the awarding gap they feel they are already at a disadvantage as the data is setting up a mindset in students and staff of inevitable failure, even though the students may be capable of academic success. A number of reports that have taken the student voice into consideration have highlighted the importance of diversifying the curriculum and the representation of Black, Asian and minority ethnic staff (for example, Stevenson, 2012; Smith, 2016).

What is challenging is discussing this issue with predominantly White colleagues on the course; there are good intentions and gestures, but no follow-through. This is because it will take finance, time and resources. The conversation starts with colleagues but the actions for change are always put to the bottom of the agenda, for easier, trendier or less uncomfortable interventions.

We try to provide extra support to Black, Asian and minority ethnic students through additional tutorials or additional discussions, (for example, regarding fieldwork). The impact is limited if the institutional infrastructure is not there to support. What is clear is that Black, Asian and minority ethnic students must not only be made to feel more included but be included to develop a more diverse curricula and thorough representation of Black, Asian and minority ethnic academics. We have heard in the past from others, you cannot be what you cannot see. If students can't see change in the awarding gap, and they do not see academics that look like them, then how can they aspire to be successful in their studies?

Change domains

Accountability and responsibility

Accountability is always the first place to go to keep an organisation's strategy in check. However, organisations must be responsible first, because a responsible organisation looks after its employees to deliver a quality service to its customers (Davis, 2016). To look after its staff and provide the necessary resources and infrastructure, staff autonomy needs to be increased, which indicates a level of trust, for example to make local decisions, and this in turn acknowledges staff expertise. Furthermore, a responsible organisation provides access to development and career progression and most importantly, has a clear and transparent vision and mission that encourages belonging at the institution level (Pink, 2009). For responsible HEIs to remain accountable and sustainable in the future, a strategic vision needs to be clearly communicated and implemented. Strategies that are clearly enacted also need to be relatable to be effective (Davis, 2016).

One of the most under-resourced and misaligned departments within HEIs are the EDI departments. These departments should be at the cornerstone of any anti-racist policy and should be key in representing all staff to meet its legal obligation of the Equality Act 2010. Key professionals need to be at the table to present high-level actions at board-level committees where important decisions are discussed and formalised. This is where workforce plans and key deliverables are actioned, signed off and measured. Boards should only sign off EDI action plans that can demonstrate thorough evidence-based literature, as well as their own demographic staff data, that actions and initiatives presented are likely to work (Kline, 2020).

Accountability metrics and reporting structures need to be clearly defined with working groups, action groups and steering committees that feed into clear strategic goals and objectives and where KPIs can be measured.[1] At present, the REC is one such indicator that requires any HEI to demonstrate the impact of clear race-specific goals and initiatives and practices that are measurable. The collection of key data on any indicator must demonstrate and update on meaningful actions to be met, both short and long term, and be reviewed annually with transparent reporting to all stakeholders, including staff and students (Kline, 2020).

Policy and procedures

The HR department in an HEI plays a very important role in the enactment of key policies and needs to be regularly reviewed. Strategic policies are central to any HEI and should be updated due to changes from the government, regulatory bodies and professional associations.

To uphold anti-racist policies and procedures for anti-racist work will be challenging, particularly if faculties or individuals fail to adhere to policies and procedures. To change the culture of the institution, it must follow through with strategic pro-action regarding service provision (CIPD, 2020). Clear, safe and separate protocols and processes are required to be laid out to meet good practices on whistle-blowing, grievances and disciplinary procedures. There must be safe, supportive and confidential spaces for staff and students to discuss racist or discriminatory issues or experiences, regardless of whether further action is required. Furthermore, a staff inclusion policy, a key policy document to establish an HEI's commitment to promoting equality of opportunity, respecting differences and providing an inclusive environment that is free from discrimination, harassment, victimisation and bullying, will be critical to uphold anti-racist policies and procedures (CIPD, 2020).

Teaching and learning strategy

The dissatisfaction with the continuing situation regarding systemic racism in HEIs has resulted in UK student-led campaigns, for example, 'why is my curriculum White?' and 'why isn't my professor Black?'[2] Current events of COVID-19 and BLM have brought to light many racial inequalities for a new generation of individuals. Students are calling for urgent implementation of changes for anti-racist actions within universities and this will in turn impact society. At present, many HEI faculty and administrative staff are still predominantly White (Tate & Bagguley, 2017; Advance HE, 2019).

Any efforts made by governments and university networks and syndicates have shown little change in the Black, Asian and Minority employment statistics, and the prevailing issue of Black, Asian and minority ethnic students' limited achievements within UK HEIs. The Black, Asian and minority ethnic attainment awarding gap is the measure of the difference in the proportion of Black, Asian and minority ethnic students achieving a first or 2:1 degree compared with their White counterparts (Universities UK and the National Union of Students, 2019). The existence of the awarding gap impacts on the job market due to the many graduate-level jobs and postgraduate opportunities that require a minimum of an upper-second-class degree (Universities UK and the National Union of Students, 2019). This means that a significant number of Black, Asian and minority ethnic graduates who leave university are excluded from a large part of the graduate employment market. The ECU Report (2018) and the Advance HE Report

(2019) show minimal change in progress, in the statistics from 2004/05 to 2016/17 for Black, Asian and minority ethnic staff and student representation, in professional services, in higher organisational positions, obtaining research contracts or successful publication rates. At the time of writing this, 0.6 per cent of UK professors are Black.

Any changes to strategies, action plans and accountability measures regarding alignment with anti-racism principles and practices will be challenging for all. The aim will be to start on a level playing field with White peers to ensure opportunities can be taken up for the benefit of all and equitable service provision without the extra burden of navigating the hurdles of racism.

Reflective questions

- Does your theory of change for the organisation reflect race EDI at its core?
- When developing your organisational or departmental strategy, did you meaningfully involve Black, Asian and minority ethnic staff, students and the local community in setting your direction?
- Do all your college/faculty-level strategies speak to the central strategy?
- Are your indicators for success meaningful when it comes to tracking the recruitment, retention and success of Black, Asian and minority ethnic staff?
- How are you benchmarking or making targets as part of your strategic goals?
- Does your strategy provide systems oversight of your institution with a race equality lens?

Notes

[1] The reader may consider a theory of change approach to integrating anti-racism into a wider strategy, accountability and planning structure: https://ideas.lifelabslearning.com/using-change-theory-to-practice-anti-racism
[2] http://www.dtmh.ucl.ac.uk/isnt-professor-black-reflection/

References

Advance HE (2019) Equality in higher education: statistical report 2018, Accessed 28 July 2020, from www.advance-he.ac.uk/knowledge-hub/equality-higher-education-statistical-report-2018

Ahmed, S. (2012) *On Being Included: Racism and Diversity in Institutional Life.* Durham: Duke University Press.

Akel, S. (2019) Insider-outsider: the role of race in shaping the experiences of black and minority ethnic students. Accessed 15 July 2020, from https://www.gold.ac.uk/media/docs/reports/Insider-Outsider-Report-191008.pdf

Akinbosede, D. (2020) Universities must be held accountable for their action on racism. Accessed 30 December 2020, from https://wonkhe.com/blogs/universities-must-be-held-accountable-for-their-action-on-racism/

Arday, J. (2015) Creating space and providing opportunities for Black, Asian and minority ethnic academics in higher education. In C. Alexander & J. Arday (eds), *Aiming Higher: Race, Inequality and Diversity in the Academy* (pp 4–42). London: Runnymede Trust. Accessed 15 July 2020, from www.runnymedetrust.org/uploads/Aiming%20 Higher.pdf

Arday, J. (2018) Understanding race and educational leadership in higher education: exploring the black and ethnic minority (BME) experience. *Management in Education*, 32(4), 192–200.

Ashong-Lamptey, J. (2016) Crafting an identity: an examination of the lived experiences of minority racial and ethnic individuals in the workplace. PhD thesis, The London School of Economics and Political Science (LSE).

Atewologun D., Cornish T. & Tresh F. (2018) Equality and human rights commission research report 113 – unconscious bias training: an assessment of the evidence for effectiveness. Accessed 28 July 2020, from https://warwick.ac.uk/services/ldc/researchers/resource_bank/unconscious_bias /ub_an_assessment_of_evidence_for_effectiveness.pdf

Berry J. & Loke, G. (2011) *Improving the Degree Attainment of Black and Minority Ethnic Students.* York and London: ECU and HEA. Accessed 15 July 2020, from www.ecu. ac.uk/wp-content/uploads/external/improvingdegree-attainment- Black, Asian and minority ethnic.pdf

Bhopal, K. (2014) The experience of BME academics in higher education: aspirations in the face of inequality, London: Leadership Foundation for Higher Education. Accessed 28 July 2020, from https://eprints.soton.ac.uk/364309/1/__soton.ac.uk_ude_personalfiles_users_kb4_mydocuments_Leadership%2520foundation%2520paper_Bhopal%2520stimuls%2520paper%2520final.pdf

Bhopal, K. (2015) *The Experiences of Black and Minority Ethnic Academics: A Comparative Study of the Unequal Academy*, Abingdon and New York: Routledge.

Bhopal, K. (2018) *White Privilege: The Myth of a Post-Racial Society*. Bristol: Policy Press.

Bhopal, K. & Henderson, H. (2019) Competing inequalities: gender versus race in higher education institutions in the UK. *Educational Review*, 73(2), 153–169. Accessed: 15 July 2020, from www.tandfonline.com/doi/abs/10.1080/00131911.2019.1642305

Bhopal, K. & Jackson, J. (2013) The experiences of Black and minority ethnic academics: multiple identities and career progression. Southampton University.

Bhopal, K. & Pitkin, C. (2020) 'Same old story, just a different policy': race and policy making in higher education in the UK. *Race Ethnicity and Education*, 23(4), 530–47. Accessed 15 July 2020, from https://www.tandfonline.com/doi/full/10.1080/13613324.2020.1718082

Bhopal, K., Brown, H. & Jackson, J. (2018) Should I stay or should I go? BME academics and the decision to leave UK higher education. In J. Arday & H. Mirza (eds), *Dismantling Race in Higher Education* (pp 125–39). Cham: Palgrave Macmillan.

Case, A. & Ngo, B. (2017) 'Do we have to call it that?' The response of neoliberal multiculturalism to college antiracism efforts. *Multicultural Perspectives*, 19(4), 215–22.

Chartered Institute of Personnel and Development (CIPD) (2020) *Developing Antiracism Strategy*, London: Chartered Institute of Personnel and Development. Accessed 28 July 2020, from www.cipd.co.uk/knowledge/fundamentals/relations/diversity/anti-racism-strategy

Colgan, F. & McKearney, A. (2012) Visibility and voice in organisations. *Equality, Diversity and Inclusion: An International Journal*, 31(4), 359–78.

Crozier, G. (2018) Race and education: meritocracy as white middle class privilege. *British Journal of Sociology of Education*, 39(8), 239–1246.

Davis, R. (2016) *Responsibility and Public Services*. Bridport, Dorset: Triarchy Press.

Denard Thomas, J., Lunsford, L. G. & Rodrigues, H. A. (2015) Early career academic staff support: evaluating mentoring. *Journal of Higher Education Policy and Management*, 37(3), 320–29.

Dorling, D. (2021) *Injustice: Why Social Inequality Persists*. Bristol: Policy Press.

Easterly, D. M. & Ricard, C. S. (2011) Conscious efforts to end unconscious bias: why women leave academic research. *Journal of Research Administration*, 42(1), 61–73.

ECU (Equality Challenge Unit) (2012) Equality Act 2010: Implications for colleges and HEIs. Accessed 15 July 2020, from https://s3.eu-west-2.amazonaws.com/assets. creode.advancehe-document-manager/documents/ecu/ equality-act-2010-briefing-revised-08-12_1584029932.pdf

ECU (Equality Challenge Unit) (2018) Equality in higher education: statistical report 2018. Accessed 15 July 2020, from https://www.advance-he.ac.uk/knowledge-hub/ equality-higher-education-statistical-report-2018

HEA (2012) Black and minority ethnic student degree retention and attainment. Accessed 15 July 2020, from www.heacademy. ac.uk/knowledge-hub/blackand-minority-ethnic-student-degree-retention-andattainment

Imperial College London (2020) How to be a white ally. Accessed 28 July 2020, from www.imperial.ac.uk/equality/ resources/how-to-be-a-White-ally

Inko-Tariah, C. (2015) *The Incredible Power of Staff Networks*. Croydon: Filament Publishing.

Iqbal, N. (2019) Academic Robin DiAngelo: 'we have to stop thinking about racism as someone who says the N-word'. *The Observer*. Accessed 20 November 2021, from www.theguardian.com/world/2019/feb/16/ white-fragility-racism-interview-robin-diangelo

Jeito Consulting (2017) Being an effective network sponsor or champion: making the most of the role. Accessed 15 July 2020, from https://media.wix.com/ugd/99032f_b75172928b92461 9ad065fc4f714f9e5.pdf

Kalev A., Dobbin F. & Kelly E. (2006) Best practices or best guesses? Assessing the efficacy of corporate affirmative action and diversity policies. *American Sociological Review*, 71(4), 589–617.

Kline R. (2020) After the speeches: what now for NHS staff race discrimination? Accessed 28 July 2020, from https://blogs.bmj. com/bmjleader/2020/06/13/after-the-speeches-what-now-for-nhs-staff-race-discrimination-by-roger-kline

Leadership Foundation for Higher Education (2017) *Academic Leadership at the Programme Level to Address the BME Attainment Gap*. London: Leadership Foundation for Higher Education.

Noon, M. (2018) Pointless diversity training: unconscious bias, new racism and agency. Accessed 15 July 2020, from www.lfhe. ac.uk/en/research-resources/researchhub/small-development-projects/sdp2017/ hertfordshire-po.cfm Employment and Society, 32(1):198-209

Pink, D. (2009) *Drive: The Surprising Truth about What Motivates Us*. Edinburgh: Cannongate.

Richardson, J. (2018) Understanding the under-attainment of ethnic minority students in UK higher education: the known knowns and the known unknowns. In J. Arday & H. Mirza (eds), *Dismantling Race in Higher Education: Racism, Whiteness and Decolonising the Academy* (pp 87–103). Cham: Palgrave Macmillan.

Rollock, N. (2019) Staying power: the career experiences and strategies of UK black female professors. Accessed 15 July 2020, from www.ucu.org.uk/media/10075/staying-power/pdf/ucu_rollock_february_2019.pdf

Rutherford, A. (2020) *How to Argue with a Racist: History, Science, Race and Reality*. London: Weidenfeld and Nicholson.

Saini, A. (2021) *Superior: The Return of Race Science*. London: Harper Collins.

Sarpong, J. (2017) *Diversify: How to Challenge Inequality and Why We Should*. London: Harper Collins.

Singh, G. (2011) *Black and Minority Ethnic (BME) Students' Participation in Higher Education: Improving Retention and Success: A Synthesis of Research Evidence.* Coventry: HEA.

Smith, S. (2016) Exploring the black and minority ethnic (BME) student attainment gap: what did it tell us? Actions to address home BME undergraduate students. *Journal of Perspectives in Applied Academic Practice*, 5(1), 48–55.

SOAS (2018) *Decolonising SOAS Learning and Teaching Toolkit for Programme and Module Convenors.* London: SOAS.

Stevens, S. (2020) Personal message from Sir Simon Stevens on Black Lives Matter and health inequalities. Accessed 28 July 2020, from www.england.nhs.uk/2020/06/personal-message-from-sir-simon-stevens-on-black-lives-matter-and-health-inequalities

Stevenson, J. (2012) An exploration of the link between minority ethnic and white students' degree attainment and views of their future 'possible selves'. *Higher Education Studies*, 2(4), 103–113. Accessed 15 July 2020, from www.ccsenet.org/journal/index.php/hes/ article/download/22576/14561

Tate, S. A. & Bagguley, P. (2017) Building the anti-racist university: next steps. *Race Ethnicity and Education*, 20(3), 289–99. DOI: 10.1080/13613324.2016.1260227.

Universities UK and the NUS (2019) Black, Asian and minority ethic attainment at UK universities: #Closingthegap. Accessed 28 July 2020, from www.universitiesuk.ac.uk/policy-and-analysis/reports/Documents/2019/Black, Asian and minority ethnic-student-attainment-uk-universities-closing-the-gap.pdf

Welton, A., Diem, S. & Carpenter, B. W. (2019) Negotiating the politics of antiracist leadership: the challenges of leading under the predominance of whiteness. *Urban Education*, 54(5), 627–30.

Wilkinson R.G. & and Pickett, K. (2009) *The Spirit Level: Why Equality is Better for Everyone,* London: Allen Lane.

PART VIII

Conclusion

19

In solidarity

Arun Verma

Introduction

When thinking about solidarity and collective action, I prime this chapter with a quote from Lilla Watson who said "if you have come here to help me, you are wasting your time. But if you have come because your liberation is bound up with mine, then let us work together" (1985).[1] This collective action is often referred to as 'allyship', whereby the notion of allyship can be defined from

> late 14c., as 'relative, kinsman' from ally (v.); mid-15c. in the sense of 'one united with another by treaty or league'. Allies as the name of the nations aligned against the Central Powers in World War I is from 1914; as the nations aligned against Germany, Italy and Japan in World War II, from 1939. (Etymonline, 2020)

In the context of anti-racism,

> Allyship is a proactive, ongoing, and incredibly difficult practice of unlearning and re-evaluating, in which a person of privilege works in solidarity and partnership with a marginalised group of people

> to help take down the systems that challenge that group's basic rights, equal access, and ability to thrive in our society. (Rochester Racial Justice Toolkit, 2020)

Examples of allyship have existed in wider equalities movements. For example, as part of the LGBTQI+ movements, there were notable increases in the number of 'out-group alliances' of non-LGBTQI+ individuals who would support this movement. This was noted through the mainstreaming of LGBTQI+ in the media (Ng, 2013) and education (Nash & Browne, 2019). There arc also examples of allyship in solidarity with people living with a disability and/or d/Deafness. For example, disabled artists have contested the stereotyped representations of disability in media narratives, and critiqued these stereotypes (for example, Hadley, 2020). Discourses of allyship in this area have focused on voice, agency and those with lived experience of disability and d/Deafness (for example, Forber-Pratt, Mueller & Andrews, 2019). Calls have been made to redefine allyship for people to reconsider their roles in shaping disability identities with references to enacting social models of disability to be authentic allies (for example, Forber-Pratt, Mueller & Andrews, 2019).

When exploring types of allies, Carlson et al (2019) refer to some of the traits of effective allies being non-self-absorbed, welcoming criticism, being accountable, listening, shutting up and reading. These traits and practices can enable allies to transition from being apathetic and unaware to more active and anti-inequality-led (Reid, 2020). In this move to a move active role in becoming anti-racist, the following change domains explore some of the areas to support our journey as a community to becoming anti-racist.

Change domains

The areas of change were identified during an online event that was hosted on allyship for race equality in universities and are a result of a community of anti-racism allies engaging in active advocacy for race equality in HE (Verma, 2020).

Leaders in solidarity

Senior leadership need to be actively advocating for the rights of racial minorities in their organisations through role modelling 'allyship' behaviours and empowering communities racialised as Black, Asian and ethnic minorities in their institutions. This should be done in reference to practising allyship behaviours noted in Carlson et al (2019) to build upon the behaviours as noted in the article and reconsidered with anti-racism in mind:

- Constant action: referring to the ability to always engage, demonstrate and commit to accountability through everyday anti-racism action.
- Embrace the intersections of oppression and privilege: recognise the intersectionality between oppression and privilege in racialised individual, interpersonal and structural relationships.
- Accountability and critical reflection: reflecting on your position as an 'ally' in your position to others, to communities and within different structures. Utilising critical reflection to inform critical action is critical to becoming anti-racist.
- Empower participation and voice: enable and empower the participation of those living at the intersection of multiple disadvantages, marginalisation and deprivation in society.
- Appreciate criticism and feedback: always strive for an open learning mindset to build knowledge and confidence in your journey to anti-racism and tackling wider inequalities.
- Be proactive: Carlson et al (2019) refer to this as 'describing privileged individuals allyship posture of learning to listen and listening to learn (Giannaki, 2016, para.12, citing Adelina Nicholls), and being self-motivated'.
- Ally is not a badge of honour: recognise that allyship and solidarity are led by actions and not by social labels.

Learning, unlearning and relearning

Unlearning, learning and evaluating one's own intersecting privileges and oppressions within the HE system can enable more authentic empathy and allyship for race equality in all aspects of universities. Such unlearning and self-reflection require allies to immerse themselves in the literature, evidence and voices of those that have raised issues concerning living within racist and colonial structures. This may be in the form of singular workshops; however, it is shown that coaching models with decision-making groups can play a significant role in creating sustainable changes for racial EDI (for example, Cooper et al, 2020).

Collective action

Racist cultures can only change when all the people within the system challenge the structure in which racism lives. To enable allies and racialised people of colour in universities to build and sustain anti-racism in university cultures, there is a need for allies to call out and address racial aggressions towards people of colour. Black, Asian and minority ethnic staff and students will continue to be minoritised, which can mean that Black, Asian and minority ethnic staff and students are not often represented in decision-making forums that can directly impact their experience, retention and success (for example, Bhopal, 2014). This means that allies need to be actively practising and doing anti-racism in spaces where they may typically be no Black, Asian and minority ethnic representation.

Formalising sponsorship and lead roles

Formalising senior leader sponsorship for Black, Asian and minority ethnic staff and student networks in institutions to demonstrate and role model race equality allyship is crucial for sustaining culture, behaviour and systemic changes in race equality in HE institutions. Sponsors should not wait to hear from their Black, Asian and minority ethnic staff or student network, but should actively seek out ways they can support the network's vision. This role modelling enables institutions to all learn from each other and take bold steps to embark on an authentic anti-racism journey. However, such sponsorship can be considered tokenistic and paying 'lip service' to race equality. To overcome these concerns, embedding mechanisms and review points with sponsors to monitor progress and success are crucial and should be agreed. Sponsors should be willing to step down if they are not able to perform and advocate for Black, Asian and minority ethnic staff and student issues at different hierarchical levels of the institution.

Reflective questions

- Have you read up on issues concerning structural, institutional and individual racism?
- When you read about White privilege and fragility, do you understand that it is to do with cultivating a more diverse and inclusive environment?
- Did you know that centring the voices of Black, Asian and minority ethnic communities when designing and delivering services will mean that you have systems and structures in place that enable everyone to thrive?
- How are you supporting and enabling your Black, Asian and minority ethnic staff and/or students' development, retention and success in HE?
- How many times have you said in a meeting that you were not comfortable with a racist comment that was made? If you don't feel like you can speak up, what will it take?

Note

[1] As referenced from a talk given at the UN Decade for Women Conference in Nairobi in 1985.

References

Bhopal, K. (2014) The experiences of BME academics in higher education: aspirations in the face of inequality. *Leadership Foundation for Higher Education Stimulus Papers*.

Carlson, J., Leek, C., Casey, E., Tolman, R. & Allen, C. (2019) What's in a name? A synthesis of 'allyship' elements from academic and activist literature. *Journal of Family Violence*, 35, 889–898. DOI: 10.1007/s10896-019-00073-z.

Cooper, J. N., Newton, A. C., Klein, M. & Jolly, S. (2020) A call for culturally responsive transformational leadership in college sport: an anti-ism approach for achieving equity and inclusion. *Frontiers in Sociology*, 5(65), 1–17. DOI: 10.3389/fsoc.2020.0006.

Etymonline.com. (2020) Ally origin and meaning of ally by online etymology dictionary. Accessed 13 October 2020, from www.etymonline.com/word/ally

Forber-Pratt, A. J., Mueller, C. O. & Andrews, E. E. (2019) Disability identity and allyship in rehabilitation psychology: sit, stand, sign, and show up. *Rehabilitation Psychology*, 64(2), 119–29. DOI: 10.1037/rep0000256.

Giannaki, A. F. (2016) The role of 'privileged' allies in the struggle for social justice. Accessed 1 February 2022, from www.humanityinaction.org/knowledgebase/724-the-role-of-privileged-allies-in-the-strugglefor-social-justice

Hadley, B. (2020) Allyship in disability arts: roles, relationships, and practices. Research in drama education. *The Journal of Applied Theatre and Performance*, 25(2), 178–94.

Nash, C. J. & Browne, K. (2019) Resisting the mainstreaming of LGBT equalities in Canadian and British schools: sex education and trans school friends. *Environment and Planning C: Politics and Space*, 39(1), 74–93. DOI: 10.1177/2399654419887970.

Ng, E. (2013) A 'post-gay' era? Media gaystreaming, homonormativity, and the politics of LGBT integration. *Communication, Culture & Critique*, 6(2), 258–83.

Reid, J. (2020) Allyship requires more than lip service – Eskalera. Accessed 13 October 2020, from https://eskalera.com/2019/04/26/allyship-requires-more-than-lip-service/

Rochester Racial Justice Toolkit (2020) Accessed 13 October 2020, from https://thetoolkit.wixsite.com/toolkit/racial-justice-101

Uluğ, Ö. M. & Tropp, L. R. (2021) Witnessing racial discrimination shapes collective action for racial justice: enhancing awareness of privilege among advantaged groups. *Journal of Applied Social Psychology*, 51(3), 248–61.

Verma, A. (2020) Allyship 'for race equality' in UK universities. Accessed 13 October 2020, from www.youtube.com/watch?v=6-6FKrxah0c&t=1618s

20

Reflections on anti-racism in higher education

Arun Verma

This anti-racism guide provides a base of key evidence and voices and translates these into intersectional areas for inquiry and change that can be integrated from strategy through to implementation in your HEI. We started this book considering the key terms and language associated with the realm and school of anti-racist thought, learning and action. There was a consideration of the current issues concerning racial identities, histories, structures, institutions and systems that all shape the experience of racism and perpetuate it in different forms and modes. The guide has outlined the core areas of the HE system relating to the staff experience, student experience, research systems, teaching systems, pedagogy and governance, strategy and operations. Each chapter and its respective sub-section has been authored by experts through professional and/or lived experiences of striving to tackle racial inequalities in what has been commonly referred to as the ivory tower, or as a university.

When exploring staff experiences, authors explored the disparities within and between academic and non-academic functions within HEIs. Each staff group have different experiences of the same system in which they may be recruited to, enabling their retention and supporting their success. Line management and supervisory capacities vary across these job functions and highlight the dissonance between a more traditional academy in furthering knowledge and scholarship, to universities that require significant business and professional staff to navigate a complex HE national and international market.

As the book progresses through to student experiences, authors talk openly and frankly about the disparities across student experience and outcomes for those in HE. One author spoke candidly about racial abuse they received while on campus and how their reporting was devalued and disempowered. Students are vital to the HE setting, and with learners coming to HE to liberate themselves and increase their success in society, our HE systems need to ensure that these students are empowered and enabled with the tools to own their success. However, structural barriers are still faced by students, and racism on campus and in learning and social spaces are increasingly prevalent, which impact their experience, learning and degree outcomes.

The research and teaching systems play a core role in profiling and raising awareness of an institution's status both nationally and on global platforms. Research and teaching excellence have entered the HE discourse, with staff pressured to achieve the best scores in such assessments and influencing students' choices and options of where they decide to pursue their degrees. Current research and teaching systems are embedded in a system of funding and grants, which can increase competition and exacerbate inequalities in outcomes for Black, Asian and minority ethnic staff. For example, the lack of funding for Black academics in the UK has an adverse impact on their security and stability in an academic career that may be in the pursuit of tenure. Clauses in teaching, research and scholarship contracts are not always reflective of the academic workload, and protected time may often become lost for staff to fulfil the increasing number of tasks, objectives and pressures placed on them by managers, departments and institutions. Black, Asian and minority ethnic staff have the additional burden of being othered in such White spaces and being subject to racial harassment on a regular basis.

Pedagogical systems were interrogated and explored by experts that considered the role and utility of decolonisation work and practice at the heart of such work. Authors strived to demystify the term decolonisation, while acknowledging the labour required to address the legacy of colonialism and imperialism in curricula and highlighting the sustainable and hopeful benefits of such work. References to large-scale decolonising programmes of work within HEIs and cross-sector working showcased that significant commitment and investment in decolonising HEIs are underway. Authors also reflected on the ways in which universities present themselves to internal and external audiences through branding and communications work, along with challenges to colonial frameworks of 'professionalism' that marginalised Black, Asian and minority ethnic communities' experience and success in HE. The chapter reflects the challenges and resistance in this journey and provides the voices of those who share the adversities of experiencing a colonial curriculum and the effect on their retention and success.

This action guide for change finally lands on exploring the role of governance, operations and strategy within HE, exploring issues pertaining to leadership, operational policy, process and strategy development, design and delivery. The focus is framed on the role of senior leaders and the lack of diversity in senior roles in HEIs. References are made to sector-wide initiatives, but there is a notable amount of consideration and action to be taken to ensure that universities undergoing extensive transformation agendas, strategic setting, delivery and operational improvement require a race equality lens, and ensuring the voices of Black, Asian and minority ethnic communities are held close to such programmes of transformational work.

Throughout the book authors have noted the critical change domains that are required for each system to lever meaningful, sustainable and penetrable changes to truly becoming anti-racist. Change domains are reflected by the extensive resources that have been signposted in references and links to guidance throughout this action book. While some change domains are similar, the reader should consider not what and how they are similar, but critically reflect on how the implementation of such change domains and recommendations require some adaptation in the part of the system where change is dictated. For example, throughout the book, authors refer to anti-racism training in different parts of the HE system. While it may be that delivering and mandating such training across an entire organisation is the solution, it's important to recognise that such anti-racism training needs to be tailored to different parts of the HE system. Anti-racism training in the realm of research systems, funding and research excellence will look vastly different to delivering it in recruitment and promotion processes and policies. The changes proposed by experts are not the only solutions to becoming anti-racist and we share these changes to provide clarity and to enable and empower you, as the reader, to be bolder, braver and more ambitious in your journey to becoming anti-racist.

This boldness and bravery require critical reflection. The questions posed throughout this guide serve to help you reconsider how you perceive the world and make sense of racism in a modernising HE sector. Some questions that were proposed in the book perhaps seem like common sense, and others may be more provocative in nature. These questions are to pose constructive discomfort and provide you with an opportunity to reimagine, relearn and reflect on your perspective, position and participation in becoming anti-racist as an individual, an institution and a sector.

What does it mean to do anti-racism in higher education?

As demonstrated throughout this book, being, doing and living anti-racism are not specific to one part of the HE system. The literature and stories throughout this action guide illustrate the complexities and multiplicities of ways in which racism manifests itself across the HE sector. Being an anti-racist means acting to tackle racism. It requires individuals, communities and institutions to be able to say 'no' to all racial aggressions. It's recognising that when a Black, Asian and minority ethnic colleague is subject to a racial injustice, that they will be supported and empowered to challenge the status quo. To be anti-racist is to truly be intersectional, and to be stronger in solidarity with those that live with multiple intersecting disadvantages, inequalities and oppressions. To be anti-racist is to be able to practice care and compassion with yourself and others. Being anti-racist offers a wholistic model to driving EEDI across one of the most influential sectors in today's society.

Examples throughout the book showcase the different opportunities to reflect, change and act in the face of racism and racial inequalities, and we invite the reader to join in solidarity and in action. What does it mean to be anti-racist? It means that you do not accept racism, inequality or injustice. It means that you are truly an enabler for a more diverse, equitable, dignified and respectful society. For institutions on this journey to anti-racism, and having read through the evidence, stories and changes noted in this book, we ask you the difficult question of 'What will your anti-racist university look like?' Becoming an anti-racist institution will enable your staff and students to be able to thrive in spaces and places where diversity is celebrated, where disparities are further narrowed, and for everyone to see diverse leaders taking the HE sector into more equitable, diverse and inclusive directions.

Index

References to endnotes show both the
page number and the note number (231n3).